CONTRIBUTORS AND CONSULTANTS

HALL BARTLETT, Ed.D., *Citizenship Education Project, Teachers College, Columbia University; Author*

WALT DISNEY, *Motion Picture and Television Producer*

EVELYN MILLIS DUVALL, Ph.D., *Author and Consultant on Family Life; Authority on Child Development*

EDNA E. EISEN, Ph.D., *Professor of Geography, Kent State University*

J. ALLEN HYNEK, Ph.D., *Associate Director, Smithsonian Astrophysical Observatory*

LELAND B. JACOBS, Ph.D., *Professor of Education, Teachers College, Columbia University*

ELEANOR M. JOHNSON, M.A., *Director of Elementary School Services, Graduate Division, Wesleyan University*

HERBERT A. LANDRY, M.S., Ph.D., *Director, Bureau of Educational Program Research and Statistics, New York City Public Schools*

MILTON LEVINE, M.D., *Associate Professor of Pediatrics, New York Hospital*

WILLY LEY, *Professor of Science, Fairleigh Dickinson University; Rocket Expert and Author*

NORMAN LLOYD, M.A., *Teacher of Literature and Materials of Music, Juilliard School of Music*

LENOX R. LOHR, M.E., D.Eng., D.Sc., *President, Museum of Science and Industry, Chicago*

WILL C. MCKERN, D.S., *Former Director, Milwaukee Public Museum; Anthropologist*

RICHARD A. MARTIN, B.S., *Curator, N. W. Harris Public School Extension, Chicago Natural History Museum*

MAURICE PATE, *Executive Director, United Nations Children's Fund (UNICEF)*

NORMAN VINCENT PEALE, D.D., LL.D., Litt.D., LH.D.; *Minister, Marble Collegiate Church, New York; Author*

RUTHERFORD PLATT, B.A., *Member of Two North Pole Expeditions with Admiral MacMillan; Author of Nature Books*

ILLA PODENDORF, M.S., *Teacher of Science, University of Chicago Laboratory Schools; Author of Science Books*

MARY M. REED, Ph.D., *Supervisor of Little Golden Books; Formerly of Teachers College, Columbia University*

JOHN R. SAUNDERS, M.A., *Chairman, Department of Public Instruction, American Museum of Natural History*

GLENN T. SEABORG, Ph.D., LL.D., D.Sc., *Chancellor and Professor of Chemistry, University of California, Berkeley; Associate Director, University of California Radiation Laboratory; Co-winner of Nobel Prize for Chemistry, 1951*

LOUIS SHORES, Ph.D., *Dean of the Library School, Florida State University; Author and Authority on Reference Materials*

NILA BANTON SMITH, Ph.B., Ph.D., *Professor of Education and Director of The Reading Institute, New York University*

BRYAN SWAN, M.S., *Teacher of Physical Science, University of Chicago Laboratory Schools; Author*

SAMUEL TERRIEN, S.T.M., Th.D., *Auburn Professor of the Old Testament, Union Theological Seminary*

JESSIE TODD, M.A., *Formerly of the Art Department, University of Chicago; Art Lecturer; Contributor to Art Magazines*

LLOYD B. URDAL, Ph.D., *Assistant Professor, School of Education, State College of Washington*

JANE WERNER WATSON, B.A., *Editor and Author of More Than a Hundred Golden Books*

WILLIAM S. WEICHERT, M.S., *Supervisor of Science, Oakland (Calif.) Public Schools*

PAUL A. WITTY, Ph.D., *Professor of Education, Northwestern University; Specialist on Gifted Children*

STAFF

ROBERT D. BEZUCHA, *Project Director;* NORMAN F. GUESS, *Editorial Director;* R. JAMES ERTEL, *Managing Editor;* PAULINE NORTON, *Assistant Project Director;* ALICE F. MARTIN, *Associate Editor. Staff Editors:* GENEVIEVE CURLEY, JOAN FALK, HESTER GELB, RICHARD D. HARKINS.

THE GOLDEN BOOK ENCYCLOPEDIA

VOLUME VIII—HUDSON TO KOREA

In Sixteen Accurate, Fact-filled Volumes Dramatically Illustrated with More Than 6,000 Color Pictures

THE ONLY ENCYCLOPEDIA FOR YOUNG GRADE-SCHOOL CHILDREN

ACCURATE AND AUTHORITATIVE

ENTERTAININGLY WRITTEN AND ILLUSTRATED TO MAKE LEARNING AN ADVENTURE

by Bertha Morris Parker

Formerly of the Laboratory Schools, University of Chicago
Research Associate, Chicago Natural History Museum

GOLDEN PRESS · NEW YORK

THIRD PRINTING, 1960

© Copyright 1959 by Golden Press, Inc. Designed and produced by Artists and Writers Press, Inc. Printed in the U.S.A. by Western Printing and Lithographing Company. Published by Golden Press, Inc., Rockefeller Center, New York 20, N.Y.

Illustrations from GOLDEN BOOKS, published by Golden Press, Inc., New York, © 1946, 1949, 1951, 1952, 1953, 1954, 1955, 1956, 1957 by Golden Press, Inc.; and from the Basic Science Education Series (Unitext), published by Row, Peterson and Company, Evanston, Illinois, © 1940, 1941, 1942, 1943, 1944, 1947, 1949, 1957, 1959 by Row, Peterson and Company.

HUDSON, HENRY (?-1611) The Hudson River is named for the English explorer Henry Hudson. So is Hudson Bay.

No date can be given for the year of Hudson's birth because no one knows exactly when he was born. Not very much is known about his early life, either.

Hudson first sailed up the river named for him in 1609. He went as far as present-day Albany. His boat was a little sailing vessel named the "Half Moon." He had been sent out by a company in Holland—the Dutch East India Company—to find a northern route to China.

Of course, Hudson found that he could not reach China by traveling up the Hudson River. The Hudson was not a strait leading to the Pacific Ocean, as he had hoped. He sailed back for Holland. During the whole trip he had trouble with his crew.

On the way back to Holland he stopped in England. There the "Half Moon" was seized, and Hudson was ordered not to go on to Holland. If he wished to go exploring, he could do so for England.

In 1610 Hudson set out again, this time in the service of England. His boat was the "Discovery." He still hoped to find a northern route to China. After a very stormy voyage, the "Discovery" came to a strait far to the north and sailed through it into Hudson Bay. On this voyage, too, Hudson had constant trouble with his men. They threatened to mutiny.

The British seized Hudson's "Half Moon."

After he reached the great bay, he began to explore it. But winter came on. The boat was stopped by ice. Hudson and his crew had to lay up for the winter.

During the long, cold winter food ran short. By spring one of the crew had persuaded most of the others to turn against Hudson. He and his small son were put in an open boat with seven crewmen. Most of these crewmen were sick. On June 21, 1611, the boat was set adrift and was lost. (See EXPLORERS.)

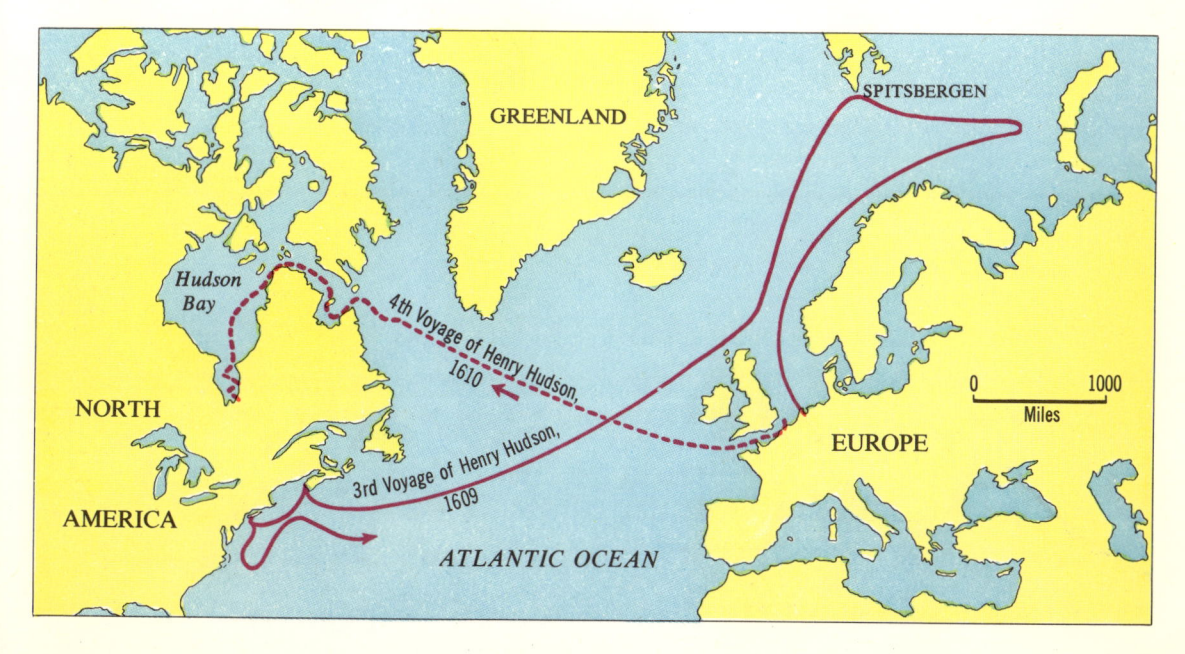

HUMMINGBIRD Ruby-throated hummingbirds are very tiny. They are only three inches long. Their beaks are almost half as long as the rest of their bodies. With their long beaks and tongues they are able to get the sweet nectar from deep down in flowers. They get many small insects along with the nectar.

Although ruby-throated hummingbirds are small, they are very good flyers. They can fly forward, backward, or straight up and down. By keeping their wings moving very fast, they can also poise in mid-air. Their feet are frail and are used only for perching on fine twigs. These tiny birds never run or even walk.

Ruby-throated hummingbirds build very firm cup-shaped nests out of plant down and other soft materials. They cover the outside with mosses and bits of bark or spiderweb. The whole nest is not much larger than half of an English walnut. The mother hummingbird lays two white eggs which are no larger than peas.

There are other kinds of hummingbirds. Some grow to be eight inches long. Some of them have red throats, some have blue, and some have black. Their bodies are mostly olive green. As is true of many kinds of birds, it is the male that wears the brighter plumage. Some hummingbirds have short bills. They drill into flowers from the side to get nectar. (See BIRDS.)

HUNGARY At the start of World War I Austria-Hungary was one of the rich and important countries of Europe. At the end of that war this great country was broken into pieces. One piece became Hungary. One became Austria. Other pieces became parts of other countries.

Since Austria and Hungary were once joined together, it might be thought that the Austrians and Hungarians are closely related. But they are not. Even their languages are different. A great many of the Hungarians are descended from a tribe that moved into Europe from Asia more than 1,000 years ago. The people of this tribe were the Magyars.

The Magyars built up a strong country. Six hundred years ago their kingdom was much larger than Hungary is now. But then the Turks became powerful and began taking land away from the Magyars. In order to have help in protecting themselves from the Turks, the Magyars allowed much of Hungary to be taken over by Austria. The people of Austria and Hungary pushed out the Turks. Later, about 100 years ago, all of Hungary and Austria were joined to

HUNGARY

form, together, Austria-Hungary.

Hungary is a farming country. The Danube River flows through it, and great plains stretch away from the Danube. In places the land is very low and swampy. In other places it is so dry that it is good only for pasture. But there is much very good farmland. Millions of bushels of corn and wheat are raised on it. It is one of Europe's chief "breadbaskets." On the grasslands hundreds of thousands of sheep and cattle are raised. Many horses are raised, too. The Hungarians are fond of horses, and some of their horses are very fine.

The country is not at all rich in valuable minerals. But it does have great stores of aluminum ore. The kind of aluminum ore found there is bauxite.

The chief city of Hungary is Budapest. This city is also Hungary's capital. Budapest is on the Danube. It was once two cities. Buda was on one side of the river, and Pest on the other. They were joined to form Budapest. Budapest used to be a gay city. Many of its visitors called it another Paris. But great damage was done to it in World War II.

It is not surprising that Hungary's biggest city is on the Danube River. Hungary has no seacoast at all. The Danube River is its only waterway to the sea. River boats helped to carry on trade with other lands and to make Budapest grow.

Since World War II Hungary has been one of the countries in which the Soviet Union has great influence. By no means do all of the Hungarians like that influence. In 1956 some of them revolted against communist ways of governing. Serious fighting took place in Budapest. Many Hungarians were killed. More than 25,000 of those who escaped came in 1957 to find homes in America. (See AUSTRIA; DANUBE RIVER; WORLD WAR I; WORLD WAR II.)

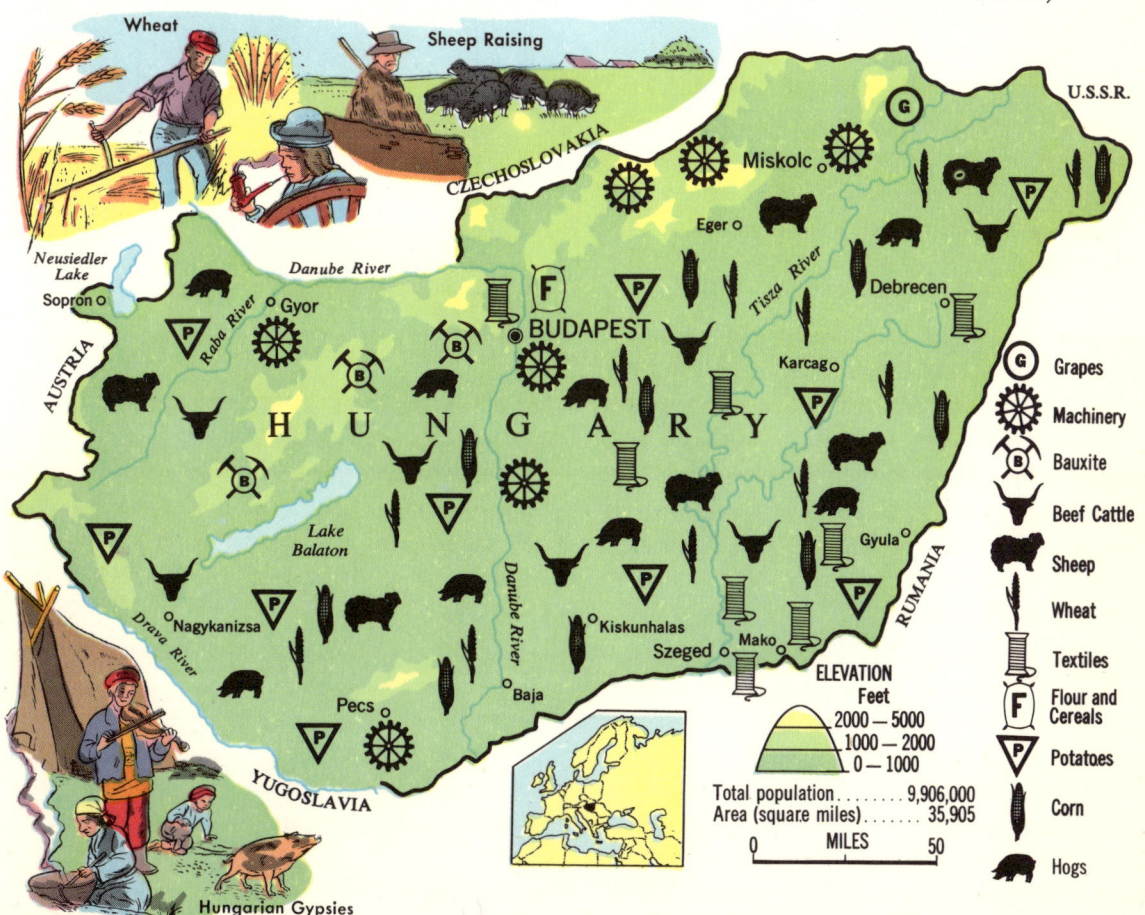

HURDY-GURDY "Here comes the man with the hurdy-gurdy!" This shout used to be one of the signs of spring. The man with the hurdy-gurdy usually had a monkey, too. After the hurdy-gurdy man played a tune, the monkey picked up coins people threw to him. Hurdy-gurdies are not as common now.

The hurdy-gurdy is hundreds of years old. The early ones had strings like a violin. The strings were inside so that they did not show. Turning the handle of the hurdy-gurdy turned a little "barrel" inside the instrument. The barrel had teeth sticking out from it. The teeth plucked the strings and played the tune.

Today's hurdy-gurdies are really hand organs. They have little organ pipes inside instead of strings. There is a barrel in them just as there was in the older hurdy-gurdies.

A hurdy-gurdy can play only the few tunes the barrel was made to play. The hurdy-gurdy man does not have to know anything about music. He is really just an organ grinder; he grinds out the tunes. (See MUSIC BOXES.)

HWANG HO The Hwang Ho is a river in China. It is 2,700 miles long, one of the ten longest rivers in the world.

"Hwang Ho" in Chinese means "yellow river." The river got its name because it carries great loads of yellow mud. It gathers this mud in the mountains and hills to the west of the great plain through which it flows to the sea.

Sometimes the Hwang Ho is called "China's sorrow." It has earned that name. Time after time it has flooded the low land on either side of it, ruining the crops growing there and making the fields too wet to be replanted for months. But the floods have also brought new soil to the plain and have helped keep the land fertile.

To help keep the river in its path, the Chinese centuries ago built dikes along it. They had to keep building the dikes higher and higher because the river kept building its bed higher by dropping part of its load of mud. Finally the bottom of the river was higher than the land on either side.

With the river bed so high, any big break in a dike was a catastrophe. More than a few times the river broke through and went racing to the sea over a new pathway.

Today the Chinese have great plans for the Hwang Ho. Forty-six dams are to be built across the river. The dams will prevent floods. They will help store up water to be used for irrigation. And the water flowing over the dams will be used to turn the generators in great power plants. Work on the dams has already been started. Soon the Hwang Ho will no longer be "China's sorrow." (See CHINA; DIKES AND LEVEES; FLOODS; RIVERS.)

HYBRIDS Some simple kinds of animals have only one parent. But most animals have two. The two parents are usually the same kind of animal. The parents of a Shetland pony, for instance, are both Shetland ponies. But a mule colt always has parents of two different kinds. Its mother is a horse and its father is a jack, or male donkey. The mule is a hybrid animal. It is a "cross" between two other animals—the horse and the donkey.

There are other animal hybrids. The zebroid is a cross between the zebra and the horse. The cattalo is a cross between the cow and the bison. Several hybrids have

HYBRIDS

been produced by crossing the zebu with different breeds of cattle.

There are plant hybrids, too. In a garden catalogue many hybrids are listed. Most of these hybrids are crosses between plants that are very much alike. Both parents of a hybrid rose are roses, but they are not the same variety. Both parents of every kind of hybrid corn are corn plants. But some plant hybrids are crosses between plants that are not so much alike. The tangelo is a cross between the tangerine and the grapefruit. The plumcot is a cross between the plum and the apricot.

It is fun to imagine what kind of animal one would get by crossing a cat and a chicken, or what kind of plant one would get by crossing an onion and a rose. But we can do nothing but imagine. For plants and animals cannot be crossed unless they are rather closely related.

Some hybrids are produced by nature. We call them chance hybrids. Other hybrids are produced by people.

The picture shows the steps in producing a hybrid rose. In a rose there are stamens that produce pollen. There is a pistil that has ovules in it. Ovules are the beginnings of seeds. Pollen grains have male cells in them. Ovules have female cells. A grain of pollen must land on the pistil and send a tube down to an ovule before the ovule can grow into a seed.

A gardener chooses the two roses he wishes to cross. He takes the stamens and the petals off of a rose on one of the rosebushes. He leaves the pistil. On it he brushes pollen from a blossom on the second rosebush. Then he covers the pistil with a paper bag so that no other pollen can reach it. The seeds that develop will have baby rose plants in them. When they grow up they will probably be like one parent in some ways and like the other parent in other ways. Hybrids might be called "living things made to order." (See BURBANK, LUTHER; POLLINATION.)

Cattalo and Offspring

PRODUCING A HYBRID ROSE

Male parent has been selected for its deep red color.

The pollen is collected from the flower of the male parent.

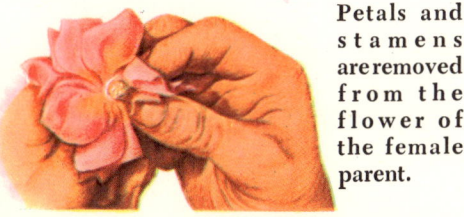

Pollen from the male parent is put on the pistil.

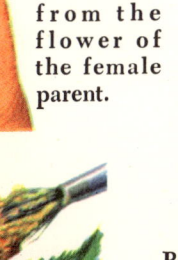

Petals and stamens are removed from the flower of the female parent.

Paper bags protect pollinated pistils.

The seed pods ripen.

HYDRAULICS

Pipe Filled with Water

Diagram of Hydraulic Auto Jack

Water Main

Hydroelectric Dam

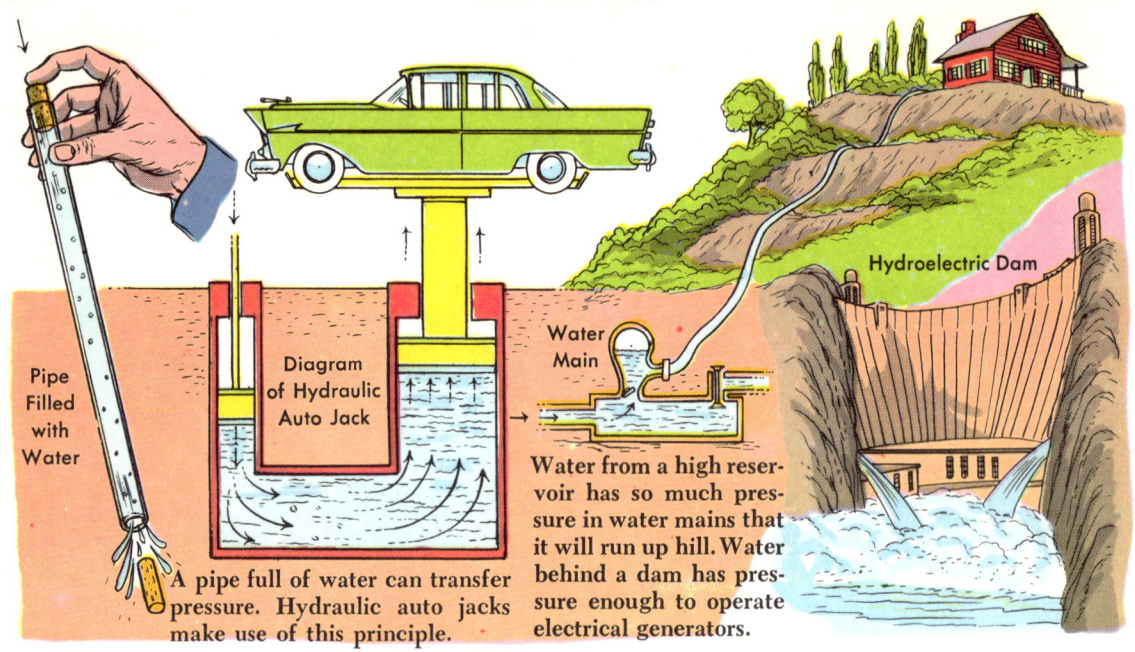

A pipe full of water can transfer pressure. Hydraulic auto jacks make use of this principle.

Water from a high reservoir has so much pressure in water mains that it will run up hill. Water behind a dam has pressure enough to operate electrical generators.

HYDRAULICS Water faucets are so common that we usually do not think about them unless they stop working. But we are able to have water piped into our homes only because men have learned how water and other liquids behave. The study of the way liquids act when they are moving or standing still is called hydraulics.

One simple fact about water that everyone knows is that water runs downhill. It can also run uphill. Imagine a container of water on a stepladder. A hose fitted in the bottom of the container runs down to the floor and then curves upward. Water will flow into the upward curve of the hose just as high as the level of water in the container. The force the water in the container exerts pushes the water up into the hose.

Engineers look for ways to get a high water level when they are planning water systems for cities. They build reservoirs on high hills so that the level of water will be higher than the tallest buildings in town. If necessary, artificial "hills" are made by building water storage tanks on high towers. Often the water is pumped up into these reservoirs or water towers and allowed to flow down from there into the city water mains.

Another fact about water and other liquids is that they easily transfer pressure. They can also be used to increase pressure. A pipe filled with water and with rubber stoppers in each end will show how liquids transfer pressure. If one stopper is forced inward, the pressure on the water will force out the stopper at the other end. If one end of the pipe were larger and had a stopper ten times as big as the stopper on the other end, the pipe would then be a machine for increasing pressure. A force of five pounds exerted on the small stopper would be increased to ten times as much, or 50 pounds, on the large stopper.

The ability of liquids to transfer pressure is used in automobile jacks. These jacks contain tanks of oil with a small stopper—called a piston—and a large one. When a man works the small piston, his force is greatly multiplied at the large piston. This piston raises the car. Hydraulic brake systems on cars are tubes filled with liquids and fitted with pistons.

Canals, flood control systems, and hydroelectric power systems are other uses of man's knowledge of hydraulics. This ancient science is being put to many useful tasks in modern life.

HYDROGEN A bottle filled with the colorless gas hydrogen looks as if it were empty. And it weighs a little less than a bottle of air would. Hydrogen is the lightest of all the chemical elements. It is the lightest material in the world!

Hydrogen is also the most abundant material in the universe. Our sun is made up largely of hydrogen, and so are the distant stars. On the earth hydrogen is rarely found by itself. There may be some very high in the atmosphere. But elsewhere it is joined with something else. It is found, as scientists say, only in compounds.

In most of its compounds hydrogen is well hidden. No one would guess by looking at a square of butter or a bowl of sugar or a glass full of water that butter and sugar and water are part hydrogen.

We are part hydrogen ourselves. So are all other animals and all plants. For living material is made partly of hydrogen. All our foods except for salt and a few other minerals are made partly of hydrogen. All the chemicals called acids have hydrogen in them. All those called bases have, too. There is hydrogen in some of the rocks in the earth's crust.

Hydrogen can be obtained easily. It can be taken out of some of the compounds it is in. Once a great deal of hydrogen was obtained for use in big balloons. It is so light that it can lift a balloon high into the air. But it is set on fire very easily, and it burns fiercely. For this reason it is no longer used for balloons that carry people. In 1937 the great dirigible "Hindenburg" burned just after it reached the United States on a trip from Germany. There were nearly 100 passengers on board. Many were killed. The accident taught everyone a sad lesson.

Today the word "hydrogen" is frightening to many people. For the hydrogen bomb is the most deadly weapon in the world. (See ACIDS AND BASES; ATOMS; BALLOONS; COMPOUNDS; ELEMENTS; HELIUM; SUN.)

HYENA The hyena is a powerful animal, but it is so timid that it is often called cowardly. Hyenas look peculiar because their front legs are longer than their hind legs. They are found in Africa and the western part of Asia.

Hyenas are meat-eating animals, but they seem to prefer the remains of animals killed by other meat eaters. They eat, for instance, the remains of zebras killed by lions. Hyenas have jaws and teeth so strong that they can crack and eat bones, even the bones of a big ox. All hyenas will eat meat so old that it is decaying. They are helpful scavengers.

The spotted hyena is also called the "laughing" hyena because it utters a wild, silly-sounding cry when it finds food. This "laugh" is heard chiefly at night, for hyenas do most of their food-hunting at night. The spotted hyena is the largest of the hyenas. It grows to be nearly four feet long. The striped hyena, as anyone would guess from its name, has stripes instead of spots. The brown hyena has on its back a light-colored mane nearly a foot long.

In zoos some hyenas have proved to be gentle. But not many people would choose hyenas as pets.

The hyena has a relative that looks much like it, but the relative is not nearly so well known. It is the aardwolf. The aardwolf, like the hyena, is a scavenger. (See SCAVENGERS.)

The large, strong hyena is a timid animal.

Patients can relive the past under hypnosis.

HYPNOTISM Long ago and in many different places the discovery was made that people can be hypnotized. A hypnotized person looks very much like a person who is walking in his sleep. He says and does what the person who hypnotized him tells him to. He may say ridiculous things he would not think of saying ordinarily. He may perform feats that he could not perform if he were not hypnotized. When a person comes out of his trance he may not remember at all what he has said or done.

A hypnotized person believes almost everything he is told. He believes that he hears sounds that he is told he is hearing. He believes he can see strange objects that he is told about.

While a person is hypnotized he may be told to do something at some time in the future. When the time comes he does what he was told to do without knowing why.

Being hypnotized does not mean losing one's will power completely. Most students of hypnotism believe that a person will do nothing which is opposed to his deeply felt ideas of right and wrong.

Anyone trained to hypnotize others is called a hypnotist. A hypnotist usually seats his patient in a darkened room. In a calm voice the hypnotist tells his patient over and over to relax and fall asleep. But not everyone can be hypnotized. And no one can be hypnotized unless he is willing.

Hypnotists sometimes give shows. They take people from the audience who offer to take part and hypnotize them. The rest of the audience has fun watching. But hypnotism is not just fun. Doctors use it in helping people who are ill. Mesmerism is an old name for hypnotism. "Mesmerism" comes from the name of a doctor, Franz Mesmer, who used hypnotism nearly 200 years ago in treating his patients.

HYRAX The hyrax lives in Africa and nearby parts of Asia. It is the "cony" of the Bible. There are a number of different kinds. Some kinds live in trees, but most kinds live among rocks in barren regions.

A hyrax is about the size of a rabbit and looks somewhat like a guinea pig. But the hyrax is not at all closely related to either of these two animals. It is more closely related to the elephant and the sea cow, but it is not a close relative of either. The hyrax really has no close relatives at all.

This small animal is a plant eater. It eats leaves and young branches of plants. During the day it rests. At dusk it starts hunting for food.

In a hyrax family there are usually from three to six babies. They are as playful as kittens. Many hyrax families live together in big communities just as prairie dogs do.

In one way a hyrax is like a skunk. It sends out a strong odor if it is disturbed.

The hyrax rests during the day and feeds after dusk.

I i

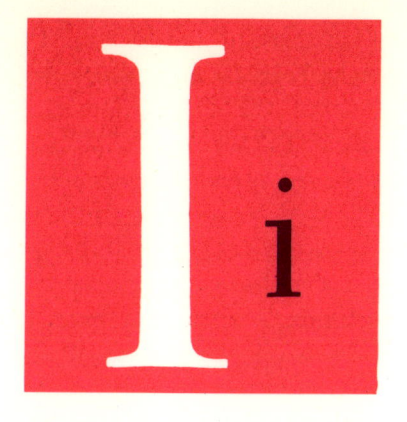

The Egyptians in their hieroglyphic writing used the picture of a hand. The makers of the first alphabet borrowed this picture. It has become the *I* of the English alphabet. The letter at first looked like a hand (ᴗ). The Phoenicians drew it without any curved lines (⌐). The Greeks simplified it (∫ , then |). The Romans usually made it as the later Greeks did, but sometimes they added a tail to it (⌡). Their two ways of writing it became our *I* and *J*.

I stands for several different sounds. It stands for four different sounds in these four words: fish, bird, mine, and machine.

ICE AGE The earth is very old. During its long history there have been many changes in climate. Between one and two million years ago one of these changes took place —the great Ice Age began.

It grew colder in the Far North. More snow fell in the winter than could melt away in the summer. The snow grew deeper and deeper. It changed to solid ice. As more snow fell, the ice grew thicker. It began to move. Great sheets of moving ice, or glaciers, were formed.

The edges of the sheets were pushed outward. At last the ice covered most of what is now Canada. And it spread southward into what is now the United States.

The ice was probably a mile deep in places. It moved over hills and valleys, rivers and forests. It moved slowly—perhaps only a foot a day. Millions of trees and other plants were buried by the ice. Many animals moved south. Among the animals able to stand the cold near the edge of the ice were mammoths, mastodons, and woolly rhinoceroses.

For thousands of years the ice moved southward. But at last the summers grew longer and warmer, and the ice began to melt back. It melted back so that most of North America was out from under it.

But again it grew colder and the ice sheets moved southward. Again it grew warmer and they melted back. Twice more the ice moved slowly southward and twice more it melted back. During the great Ice Age much of Europe, too, was covered with ice. The ice sheets left many calling cards behind them. They gouged deep scratches in the rock they moved over. They cut off the tops of hills and widened valleys. They pushed along great piles of soil, which remained behind when the ice melted back. They left huge boulders perched in places where only ice could have put them.

Scientists now know that the great Ice Age was not the only ice age in the earth's history. Millions of years earlier there were

The woolly rhinoceros had protective fur.

other ice ages. The ice may possibly come again some day, too.

In fact, scientists are not sure that the great Ice Age is really over. There have not been very many thousand years since the last retreat of the ice. But there are no signs that it is getting colder in the Far North. The glaciers that are still there are not spreading. (See CAVE MEN; EARTH HISTORY; FIORDS; GLACIERS; GREENLAND; MAMMALS OF YESTERDAY.)

ICEBERGS

Polar bears swim in the cold, ice-filled Arctic waters.

ICEBERGS Glaciers are great sheets or rivers of ice. They move very slowly. In many places in the Far North and the Far South they reach the sea. When the ice pushes past the edge of the water, huge pieces break off and float away. These floating pieces are called icebergs.

"Iceberg" means "mountain of ice." In the far south there are icebergs several miles across and as tall as a 50-story building. Some of the northern icebergs are a mile across and 100 feet high. Many of them come from the icecap that covers most of Greenland.

As icebergs float into warmer waters, they gradually melt. But an iceberg may travel for 2,000 miles before it disappears.

In the sunshine all the colors of the rainbow may be seen in an iceberg. In many icebergs there are caves that have been carved out by the waves. These caves look dark purple. At night icebergs look ghostly white as they move through the water.

Icebergs are a danger to ships. In a fog it is easy for a ship to have a head-on collision with one. A ship, moreover, may be wrecked by an iceberg even if the ship seems to have plenty of room to pass. The reason is that there is eight or nine times as much of an iceberg below the water as above it. The part hidden underwater may spread out into a great shelf of ice.

One of the worst shipwrecks of this century was caused by an iceberg. In 1912 the "Titanic," the biggest passenger ship that had ever been built, was sunk by an iceberg in the North Atlantic. More than 1,500 lives were lost. As a result of this shipwreck the International Ice Patrol was formed. This patrol reports icebergs in Atlantic shipping lanes. (See GLACIERS.)

Icebergs are dangerous to ships because most of their bulk is below the surface of the water.

The "Titanic" was sunk by an iceberg.

Cutters sail in northern waters on ice patrols.

ICE CREAM

Making Ice Cream with an Old-fashioned Ice Cream Maker — *Ice Cream Bar* — *Strawberry Sundae* — *Hot Fudge Sundae* — *Ice Cream Cone* — *Ice Cream Man* — *Banana Split*

ICE CREAM Frozen desserts are not new. More than 600 years ago Marco Polo brought home from the Far East recipes for ices made with fruit juices. But ice cream is much newer. No one knows when or where it was first made. We do know that Dolly Madison, the wife of the fourth president of the United States, served ice cream at a party in the early 1800's. We know too, that it was first made on a big scale in Baltimore in 1851. Now ice cream has become one of the best-liked foods in America. Americans eat about three billion quarts a year.

Ice cream not only tastes good, but is also one of the most nourishing foods we eat. It is more than three-fourths milk and cream. It always has sugar and flavoring in it. It may have fruit, nuts, egg, and gelatin in it, too. The egg and gelatin make it smooth. There are a great many flavors of ice cream. Vanilla is the most popular. Then come chocolate, strawberry, and butter pecan. One big chain of restaurants advertises that it makes and sells 40 different flavors of ice cream.

At first all ice cream was made at home. It was made in small freezers. The mixture to be frozen was put in a metal can inside a wooden bucket. Chopped ice mixed with salt was packed in the bucket around the can. A crank turned a paddle inside the can. This paddle kept stirring the mixture so that it would freeze evenly.

Some ice cream is still made at home in this way. Some is made in the ice trays of refrigerators. But most ice cream today is made in big ice cream plants. Big milk trucks bring the milk and cream to the plant. Other trucks bring sugar and the other materials to be used in the ice cream. Nuts, fruits, and flavorings are brought from all over the world.

First a "mix" is made of all the materials except the fruits and nuts. This is pasteurized in great tanks to make sure there will be no harmful bacteria in it. The mix next goes to tanks where the fat particles are broken up; we say it is homogenized. It is then ready for the freezer. When the mix is partly frozen the fruit and nuts, if there are to be any, are added. Air is whipped into the ice cream as it freezes. The frozen ice cream goes to a very cold hardening room for a few hours. When it comes out it is ready for sale.

Much ice cream is eaten plain as a dessert at meals. But a great deal goes into ice cream cones, milk shakes, ice cream sodas, sundaes, and ice cream bars. Some goes into such fancy desserts as parfaits and pie alamode. How we would miss ice cream if we had to do without it! (See DAIRYING; FLAVORING; FOODS; MILK.)

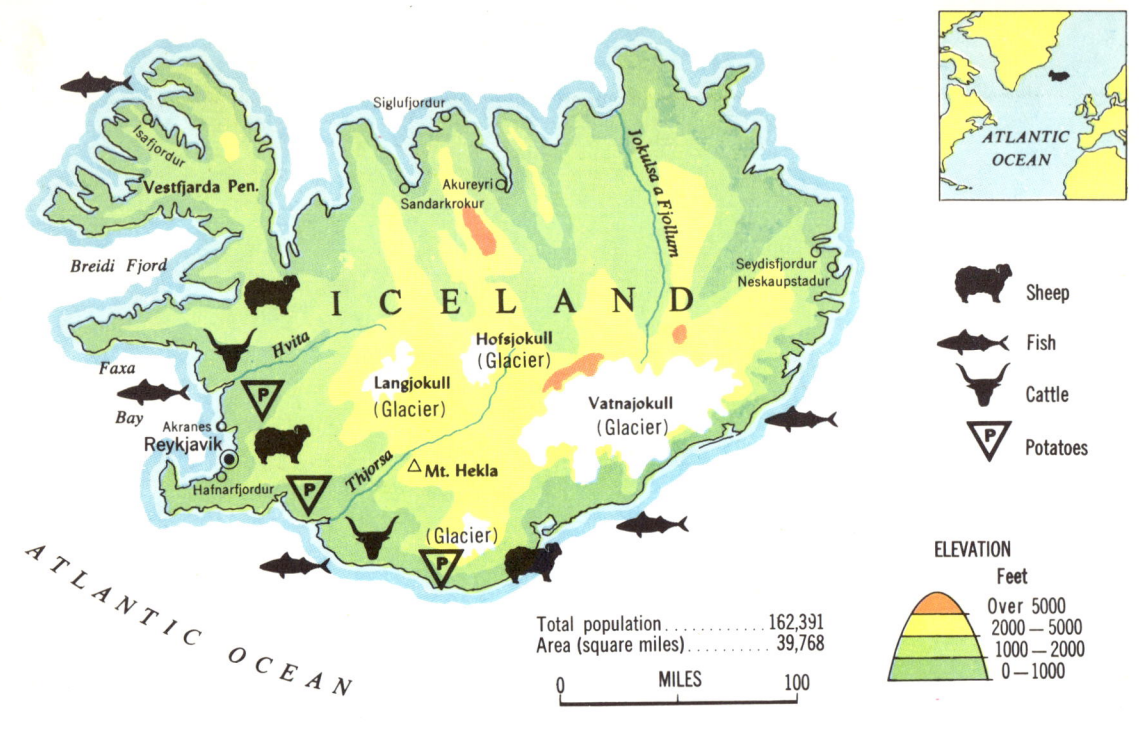

ICELAND The Norsemen were great sailors. Long before Columbus reached America, Norsemen had sailed far enough out into the big Atlantic to reach the island of Iceland. Iceland was settled more than 1,000 years ago.

There is much ice in Iceland. About an eighth of the island is covered with snowfields or glaciers. And, surprisingly, Iceland is a land of hot springs, too. There are hot springs in Iceland because it has many volcanoes. The island is only about the size of Kentucky. But in the last 500 years about a third of all the lava that has poured out from all the volcanoes on the earth has come from the volcanoes of Iceland.

Iceland's snowfields and glaciers are on a mountainous plateau which is almost as big as the island. In the rivers that flow from central Iceland to its coast there are many falls. Most of Iceland's people live on or very near its coast. Reykjavík, its capital and only city, is a seaport.

Homes and other buildings in Reykjavík are heated by water piped to them from hot springs. Power from waterfalls is used in making electricity which lights nearly all the homes in Iceland. Iceland has no railroads. But good auto roads that run near the coast connect most of the towns. Planes that fly over the plateau make regular trips between Reykjavík and several towns.

Iceland has only about the same number of people as the city of Spokane, Wash. Many of them are fishermen or sheep farmers. Two things which Iceland sends to other lands are fish and cod-liver oil. Hay for sheep, cattle, and ponies is the chief farm crop. Potatoes and turnips are also raised. Except on the plateau, winters are not very cold. Iceland's summers are cool.

Iceland is famous for the many books, magazines, and newspapers printed there. All Iceland's children go to school. They read many stories of heroes of long ago.

For centuries Iceland was part of Denmark. Now it is independent. In 1930 Iceland celebrated the 1,000th birthday of its lawmaking group, which is called the Althing. Iceland's Althing is the oldest of all the lawmaking groups in the nations of the world today. (See DENMARK; GLACIERS; GULF STREAM; HOT SPRINGS; ISLAND; VIKINGS; VOLCANOES.)

ICE SKATING Children in many parts of the world ask for ice skates at Christmas time. Ice skates have been popular for many centuries.

As one would guess, skating on ice first became popular in countries that have long, cold winters. At least 1,000 years ago the people of what are now Norway, Denmark, and Sweden were skating on runners of bone. Ancient books tell us that skating had become a sport in England by the time of the Crusades.

Ice skating was probably used first as a means of getting from one place to another. A man on skates can go twice as fast as a good runner. Today ice skating is a sport and has a place in the Olympic games.

Many people go ice skating just for the fun and the exercise. Some others take part in ice skating contests. There are ice skating races and figure skating contests. Special steel skates have been developed for speed skating and figure skating as well as for ice hockey players.

Figure skating is a sport that takes great skill and many hours of practice. The skater must perform according to an exact pattern. The *figure-eight* is one of the simplest patterns and is usually the first one a figure skater learns. The grace and beauty of figure skating make it pleasing to watch. (See GAMES AND SPORTS; OLYMPIC GAMES; WINTER SPORTS.)

Children Skating to School on Holland's Frozen Canals

The ichneumon fly helps the farmer by eating insects.

ICHNEUMON FLY Very few people recognize an ichneumon fly when they see one. But ichneumon flies are quite important. They are among our insect helpers. By laying their eggs in or near the eggs or caterpillars of harmful insects, they help us get rid of these insects. The larvas of the ichneumon flies, as soon as they hatch, begin to eat up the eggs and caterpillars that are near by.

There are many kinds of ichneumon flies. Some measure several inches from the head to the tip of the long egg-laying tube. Some are almost too small to be seen without a microscope.

The ichneumon fly pictured is called the long-tailed ichneumon. It is one of the largest in the group. Its long egg-laying tube looks fragile, but the insect can push it deep into solid wood.

Ichneumon flies are not true flies. They are relatives of the wasps, bees, and ants instead. In fact, they are often called ichneumon wasps. All the wasps, bees, and ants are believed to have come from insects very much like the ichneumon flies of today—insects that lived more than 60 million years ago. (See ANTS; BEE; INSECTS; WASPS.)

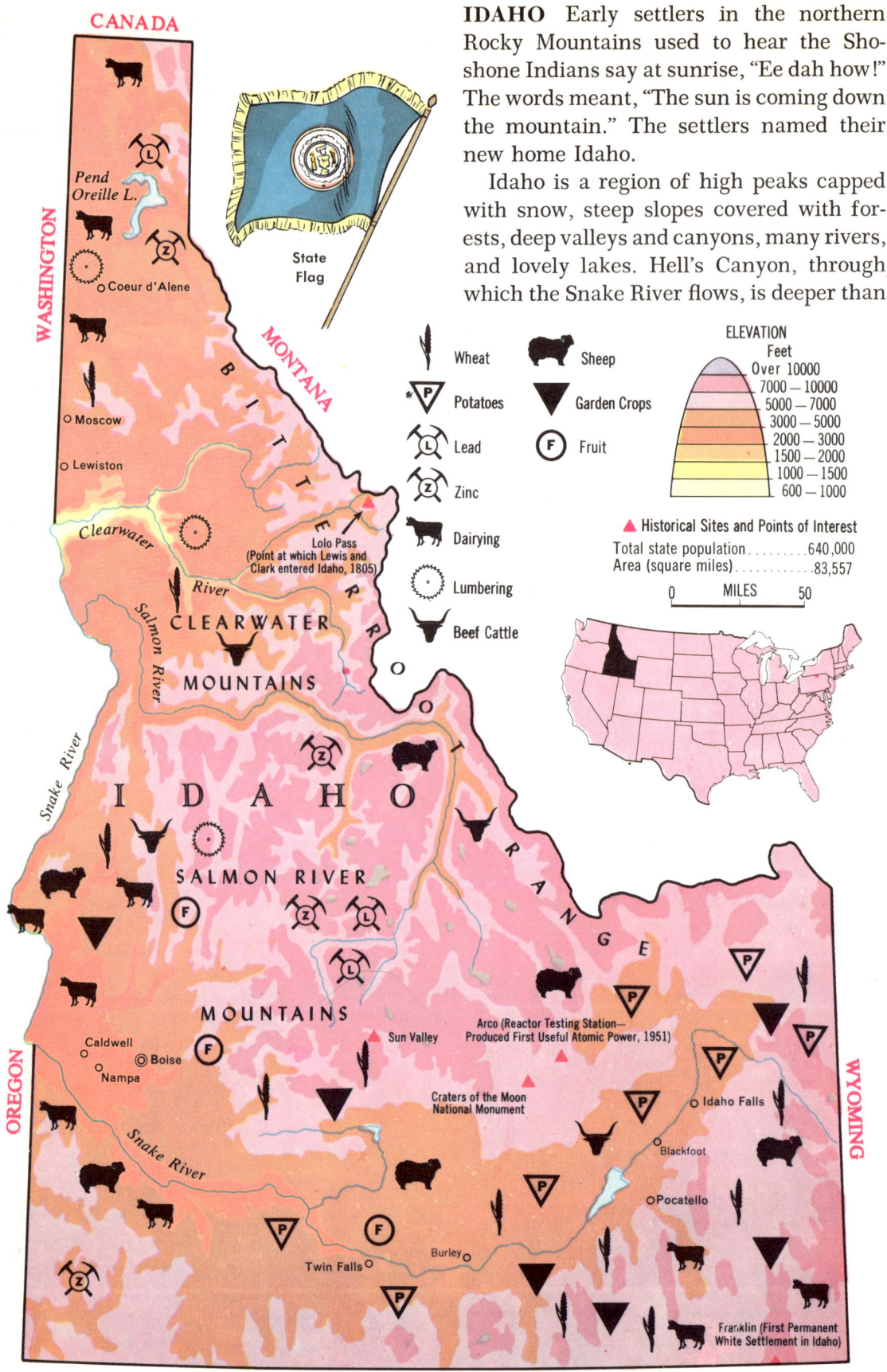

IDAHO Early settlers in the northern Rocky Mountains used to hear the Shoshone Indians say at sunrise, "Ee dah how!" The words meant, "The sun is coming down the mountain." The settlers named their new home Idaho.

Idaho is a region of high peaks capped with snow, steep slopes covered with forests, deep valleys and canyons, many rivers, and lovely lakes. Hell's Canyon, through which the Snake River flows, is deeper than the Grand Canyon of the Colorado. The Shoshone Falls are higher than Niagara Falls. Hot springs and great stretches of hardened lava tell that there were once volcanoes here. The United States Government has set aside a lava field as the Craters of the Moon National Monument.

The state is now a popular vacation land for skiers, campers, fishermen, and big-game hunters. Sun Valley, in southern Idaho, is a famous resort spot.

Idaho is a big state. Only 13 states are larger. But it does not have a big population. More than 40 states have more people. The capital, Boise (BOY see), is Idaho's largest city. It has only about 35,000 people in it. There are six other cities that have more than 12,000 people: Pocatello, Idaho Falls, Twin Falls, Nampa, Lewiston, and Coeur d'Alene (kor dal AYN).

In spite of mountains and much dry land, farming is the chief occupation of the people of Idaho. Irrigation has turned sagebrush wastes into fertile crop land. The largest farming region of the state is along the Snake River and its branches. The most famous of the irrigated crops is the Idaho potato. Only one state—Maine—produces more potatoes than Idaho. Wheat, which grows without irrigation, is the most valuable farm crop.

Many ranchmen raise livestock in Idaho, especially in the Snake Valley. The beef cattle graze on the lowland pastures. The sheep graze there too, but move to mountain pastures in the summer. Some of the ranches extend over several thousand acres of land. In southeastern Idaho many farmers are in the dairy business. They ship milk to nearby cheese factories. Pocatello cheese is well known in many distant markets.

In the state there are some flour mills and beet sugar factories. At Lewiston there is a large plant which freezes fruit to ship to market. Sawmills are as widespread as forests. The world's largest mill for sawing white-pine lumber is at Lewiston.

Idaho is rich in minerals. It leads all the states in the mining of zinc and silver. Near Coeur d'Alene, in northern Idaho, is the largest silver mine in the United States. Phosphate mining has also become important in recent years.

The first Americans to visit the Idaho country were a band of exploring frontiersmen led by Meriwether Lewis and William Clark in 1805. Fur trappers, fur traders, and missionaries were the first settlers. The discovery of gold in 1860 hastened settlement. Mining towns such as Lewiston, Boise, and Coeur d'Alene sprang up. The coming of the western railroads and the development of irrigation systems helped to bring more people into the area. In 1890 Idaho became the 43rd state of the United States.

Idaho made a name for itself in 1951. In the desert laboratory at Arco, in southern Idaho, atomic energy was used for the first time to produce electricity.

ILLINOIS

ILLINOIS

ILLINOIS This north central state takes its name from the tribe of Indians called Illini, a word meaning "man." Man has built a fine state on the old Indian hunting grounds. The huge city of Chicago spreads out along the southwestern shores of Lake Michigan. Land and water routes connect this busy section of the state with the Mississippi River on Illinois' long western border, and also with the Ohio River, the southern boundary of the state.

In the early 1800's pioneer farmers from Kentucky, Tennessee, and the Carolinas settled in the forest regions of southern Illinois. Later, pioneers from the northeast came by lake boats to settle in the forests of northern Illinois. Between the northern and southern settlements stretched a vast extent of level land covered with tall grass. It was so tall in late summer that it reached up to the saddle of the farmer's horse. Only along the streams was there woodland on these prairies. Illinois is known even today as the Prairie State.

The pioneers had never before seen prairies. They feared to build homes on them because of the lack of timber, the danger of raging grass fires, and the high winds. They thought that prairie soil was not fertile. Later, however, the settlers found prairie soil to be very rich.

Illinois prairies are now among the richest farmlands of the world. Here, where summers are hot and rainy, farmers raise corn and soybeans. They feed hogs, cattle, and dairy cows. Illinois stands first among the states in soybean production and high in other crops and livestock.

The factories and mills of Illinois bring in several times the wealth gained by the farms. It is among the five top-ranking states in manufacturing. The farms aid the factories. They provide raw materials. Farmers buy factory goods. Farm machinery is made in many factories. Other factories use corn to make starch, syrup, and whisky. Still others buy soybeans to produce oil, meal, and paint. The Chicago district leads in manufacturing. It produces much steel. It has large oil refineries and meat-packing plants. Locomotives, railroad cars, and books and magazines are a few of the many things manufactured here. Other manufacturing cities are Peoria, Rockford, East St. Louis, Springfield, Decatur, Aurora, Elgin, Moline, and Joliet.

Strip coal mines and oil wells provide much of the fuel needed. Freight cars, trucks, and river barges carry goods over the dense rail, highway, and river network. Great Lakes carriers bring iron ore to the steel mills and carry grain east. The many air lines that serve Illinois are also vital to the work of the state.

Illinois ranks only 24th in size. But it has a large population, the 4th in the country. It had an early start. In 1699 the first town was settled at Cahokia. During the Revolutionary War George Rogers Clark and pioneer soldiers helped to gain Illinois and other territory for the United States.

In 1818 Illinois became the 21st state. Abraham Lincoln played an important part in the story of Illinois. While he was living in Springfield he was one of a group that succeeded in having the state capital moved there from Vandalia. In central Illinois are many things to remind one of Abraham Lincoln and help explain why the state is often called "The Land of Lincoln."

Hog Raising

Strip Mining Coal

Corn

Cattle Market

New Salem State Park "The Lincoln Village"

IMMIGRATION "Migration" means "traveling." "Immigration" means "traveling into a new country."

It is not always possible for a person to move to a new country. His own country may not let him leave, and the one he wants to enter may not let him in.

For many years the United States welcomed everyone who wished to come to live there. But the time came when so many people wanted to come from some of the world's very crowded countries that it seemed wise to set some limits.

Now the United States has immigration quotas. Each year only so many people may come in from another country. Even those for whom there is room are looked over carefully before they are allowed to enter. The United States does not allow anyone to come in who has a contagious disease. It does not allow anyone to come in who shows signs that he will not be able to learn American ways. Criminals and people who might try to overthrow the government are shut out. Very old or very young people are allowed to enter only if there is someone in America who promises to look after them.

A great many immigrants coming from Europe into the United States used to have to stop at Ellis Island in New York's harbor to be inspected. Now most of the inspection is done on shipboard.

Many people talk of being an immigrant as if it were something in a person's disfavor. This idea is very wrong. Except for the Indians, all the people in the United States are either immigrants or descendants of immigrants. Even the Indians are descendants of people who are thought to have migrated into the Americas from Asia long ago. (See CITIZENSHIP.)

IMPALA The impala is an antelope. All antelopes can leap over the ground very fast. The impala is one of the fastest. It is also one of the most graceful.

Hunters say that no animal can get into motion more quickly than the impala. A hunter may come upon a herd of impalas quietly eating grass. The next instant they will move off in great leaps and bounds.

Impalas are found wild only in Africa, but there are some in zoos in other lands. They are not easy to catch, for they can leap over almost any net set for them. After they are caught, impalas are hard to ship, for their legs are so slender that they break easily. And they are hard to keep penned up in a zoo, for they can jump almost any fence. (See HOOFED ANIMALS.)

The impala is one of Africa's fastest and most graceful animals.

Pizarro was a cruel invader.

INCAS In 1950 newspaper headlines told about an earthquake that had destroyed the city of Cuzco in Peru. To the people who knew the story of the Americas before the days of Columbus, this news meant that the capital of the once-great empire of the Incas was in ruins.

The Incas were Indians. Their empire once stretched from what is now Ecuador along the west coast of South America through Peru and Bolivia into Chile. Much of it was in the high Andes Mountains. The capital, Cuzco, was two miles above the sea. There were many other Inca cities.

The Incas were at their height in South America when the Aztecs were at their height in Mexico. The Inca empire fell to the Spanish conqueror Pizarro a few years after the Aztecs had fallen to Cortés.

The Incas were remarkable builders. They used blocks of granite in their buildings. Some of these blocks weighed more than 100 tons, and some were carried many miles from where they were quarried. How, without machines or horses or oxen, and working only with tools of stone, they could cut them, take them to where they were wanted, and lift them into place is a mystery. The Incas used no mortar. But they cut and fitted their blocks of stone together so well that there was no room for even a knife blade between them.

The Incas built palaces and temples and such wonderful fortresses that the Spaniards called one of them the "Eighth Wonder of the World." They also built fine roads along the mountainsides. One was 1,500 miles long. Suspension bridges carried the road over deep gorges. Runners sped along these roads carrying messages.

The Inca builders also built terraces on the mountainsides so that barren mountain slopes became gardens. They built reservoirs, too, and irrigation ditches to carry water to their farms and gardens.

The ruins left by the 1950 earthquake showed what good builders the Incas were. Walls that had been built by them still stood, while later ones were destroyed.

The Incas were far ahead of the other Indians of their time in another way. They had domesticated animals. They had tamed both the llama and the alpaca. These two animals made good "pack horses."

Our common white potato is often called the Irish potato. Inca potato would be a better name for it. For its original home is Peru. The Incas were raising "Irish" pota-

The Inca promised Pizarro a pile of gold as high as his arm could reach.

toes and also corn when the Spaniards reached the New World.

The Incas could not write. They kept some of their records by tying knots in cords. Their knotted cords are called quipus. Although the Incas could not write, they did excellent weaving and made beautiful pottery. They had trumpets and flutes and probably other musical instruments.

Inca priests knew a great deal about the sun and the planets and the stars. It is not surprising that they did, for the Incas were sun worshipers. A temple to the sun in Cuzco was covered with gold. Gold, they said, came from tears of the sun.

The ruler of the Incas was called the Inca. His people thought of him as a god. The Inca had a fabulous store of gold. One story is that the Inca covered his body with a layer of powdered gold once every year and then went out into Lake Titicaca to wash it off. It was, of course, lost in the lake. Another story tells that the "fence" around the plaza in the center of Cuzco was a heavy gold chain. It was thrown into a lake to save it when the Spanish conquerors came and has never been recovered.

The story of the conquering of the Incas is one of the dark chapters in the story of the settling of the Americas. Pizarro was a cruel Spaniard who cared for nothing but the Inca's gold. To get it he ruined a civilization that had flourished for 500 years. When Pizarro reached Cuzco he made the Inca a prisoner. The Inca offered a ransom. He reached his hand up as high as he could and made a mark on the wall of his prison room. As his ransom he would fill the room up to that mark with gold. Pizarro accepted the offer and the gold poured in. But after the ransom was paid, the Inca was killed.

Cuzco was badly damaged not only by Spaniards but by the Incas themselves when they fought fiercely to drive the Spaniards out. The earthquake only did over again what had been done more than 400 years before. (See AZTECS; HISTORY; MAYAS; PERU.)

INCUBATOR A chicken egg in order to hatch must be kept warm. A mother hen sits on her eggs to hatch them. Her body keeps them just warm enough. But many little chickens are hatched from eggs that were kept warm in a different way. The eggs were kept warm in an incubator. Ducks and turkeys and even game birds are sometimes hatched in incubators, too.

An incubator is a kind of oven. The first incubators were heated with oil lamps and had to be watched carefully. There was danger that they would get too warm or too cool. Most incubators today are heated with electricity. It is easy to keep them at an even temperature. For chickens, the temperature should be kept at about 102°F. The eggs are turned from time to time so that they are heated evenly all over. The air inside the incubator must be kept fresh and moist as well as warm.

Incubators of another kind are found in hospitals. They are for babies that are especially tiny and weak when they are born. These babies need to be kept as warm as they were when they were still in their mothers' bodies. As a rule they are soon big and strong enough to leave the incubators. Incubators, now that they are in common use in hospitals, are saving the lives of a great many babies.

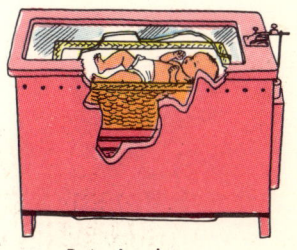

Egg Incubators

Baby Incubator

INDIA

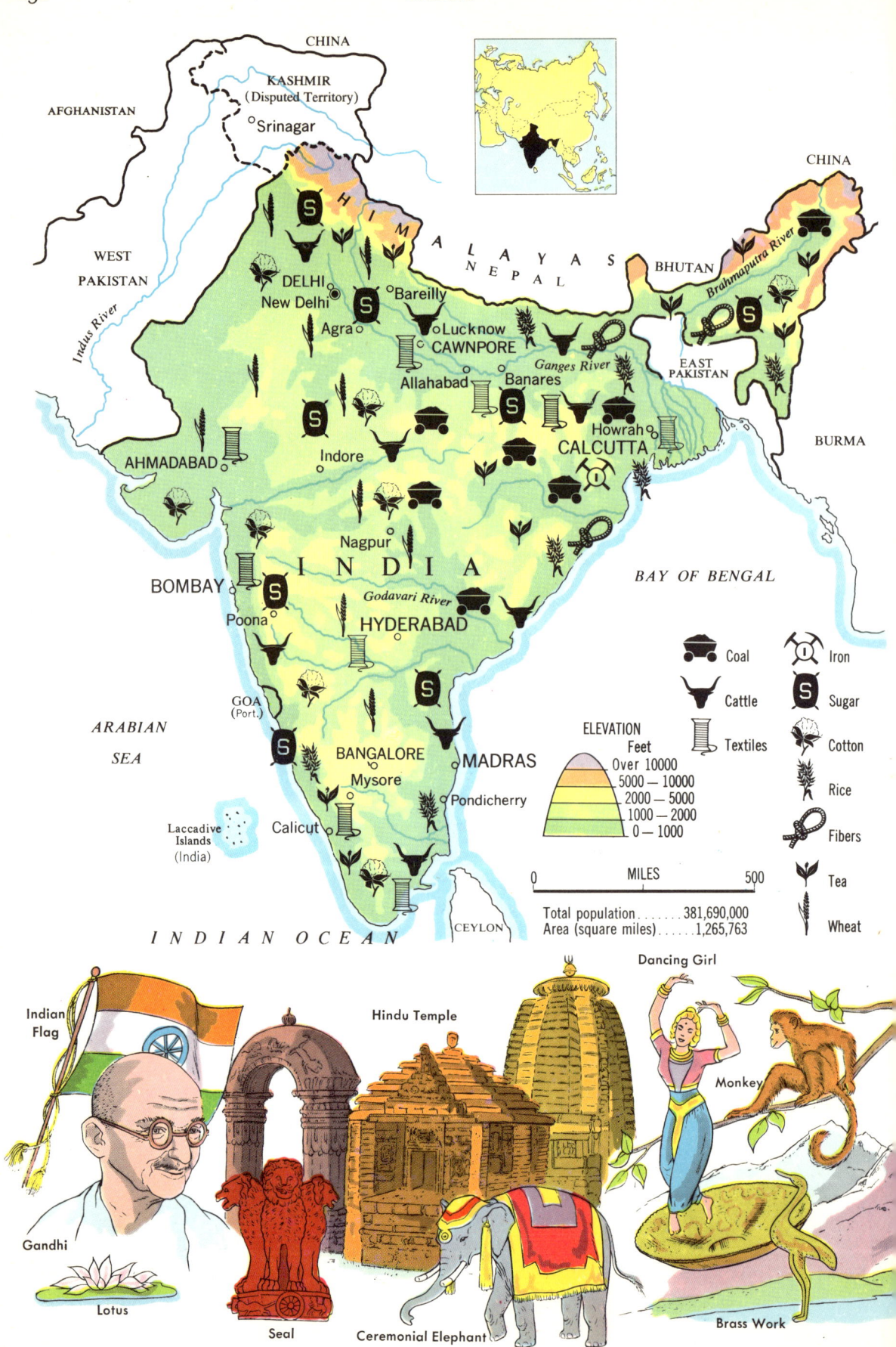

INDIA

INDIA As most people know, India is a big, very warm land far from the United States. Suppose an airplane were to make the shortest possible trip to the heart of India from St. Paul or Denver or Omaha. Strange as it may seem, the plane would fly over the North Pole! Places in the heart of India are just halfway round the world from those cities. With a string and a globe it is easy to see that the shortest route between central India and any of those cities crosses the Pole.

The Republic of India is new. It spreads over most of what was British India. But the British gave up their control of the government of India in 1947. At that time the Hindu and Moslem people in India decided to have separate countries. Now the one in which most of the people are Hindus is the Republic of India. The other one, where most of the people are Moslems, is Pakistan. Only six countries are larger than the new India. But it is a crowded land. One out of every eight people in the world lives in it.

Many things in new India are newer than the republic. Among them there are schools, factories, and one of the world's greatest dams. There are still some things that were there long before early British traders reached India. Most things in the new republic were there before 1947. Among them are hundreds of thousands of farm villages. The following word picture of one of these villages gives some idea of the life of millions of the people who live in crowded India:

Smoke is rising from the cooking fires outside the mud-brick homes. The mothers stir pots of rice and vegetables. For supper there may also be milk from the family cow or goats. The children have gathered dried cattle manure for fuel. And in the fields they have helped to scare birds away from newly cut grain. As the sun sets, men come from the fields carrying their wooden farm tools. Oxen draw home small carts of harvested grain. Tomorrow, on the village threshing floor, their heavy hoofs will pound from that grain the precious seeds. The village potter and shopkeeper close their stalls. It will soon be bedtime.

The great Himalaya Mountains border northern India. Some tea is raised on their lower slopes. But on those slopes there is also much jungle in which tigers and other wild animals live. A very wide lowland belt of good farmland stretches all the way across northern India. Many millions of India's farmers live in this vast lowland in which the great Ganges River flows eastward. Millions of other farms are here and there on the higher land south of that lowland and in the strips of lowland along the coast. The chief food crops in India as a whole are rice, wheat, and millet. The main crops for use in India's textile mills and for export are cotton and jute.

In India's big ports of Calcutta, Bombay, and Madras, and in its other cities, are many wealthy, highly educated Hindus. Many young Hindus study first in Indian universities and then abroad. Gandhi and his follower Nehru, both great leaders, deserve much credit for the big changes now going on. New ways of helping India's farmers are being worked out. Big new steel mills to use more of India's riches in coal and iron are being built. There are many textile mills. Progress of many kinds is being made in this great new republic.
(See BOMBAY; CALCUTTA; HIMALAYAS.)

INDIANA "The Crossroads of America" is a fitting motto for this rather small state. The National Road, begun in 1815, ran across central Indiana. This government-built road was used by thousands of settlers' wagons and by stagecoaches carrying passengers and mail. It is now U.S. 40. The main railroad lines between Chicago and New York cross northern Indiana. The Indiana Turnpike is a vital link in the expressways between Chicago and New York.

Indiana, or "Land of the Indians," is called the Hoosier State. It is 38th in size, but 12th in population. This north-central state touches Lake Michigan on the northwest. Its lake-shore cities merge with the huge city of Chicago. The Wabash River forms part of Indiana's western border. The Ohio River is its southern boundary.

French explorers and fur traders opened up the Indiana country. Their first settlement was at Vincennes about 1732. After the Revolutionary War, farmers from the South and East came and made small clearings in the forests. In 1816 Indiana became the 19th state in the Union. Its constitution was the first to provide for the setting up of public schools for all children.

Today much of Indiana is covered by fine farmlands. The northern two-thirds of the state is almost level and has rich soil. The hot, rainy summers help to produce good crops of corn and other grains. These are used to fatten livestock. Some farmers have huge sprays to water their fields if the rainfall does not come as needed. Some special crops such as spearmint and peppermint are grown. In the hilly country along the Ohio River there are many fruit orchards and tobacco fields.

Indiana has many vacation spots. The beauty of the hills, woods, and rivers attracts artists and tourists in spring and fall. Many lakes in wooded areas in the north provide good swimming, boating, and fishing. The sand dunes along Indiana's lake shore are world famous. The mineral springs in the south are popular resorts.

Indiana's Bedford limestone is famous for its high quality as a building stone. It is quarried in the southeastern part of the state. Indiana also has much soft coal.

The cities on the shore of Lake Michigan are Indiana's share of one of the world's great centers for producing iron and steel, and petroleum products. One of the world's largest steel plants is at Gary.

Indianapolis, the capital and largest city, is a center of manufacturing and trade. Once a year—on Memorial Day—a famous 500-mile auto race takes place there. Indiana ranks high in the manufacture of automobile parts, airplane engines, farm machinery, and musical instruments. Four cities besides Indianapolis have more than 100,000 people. They are Gary, Fort Wayne, Evansville, and South Bend. (See CORN BELT; DUNES.)

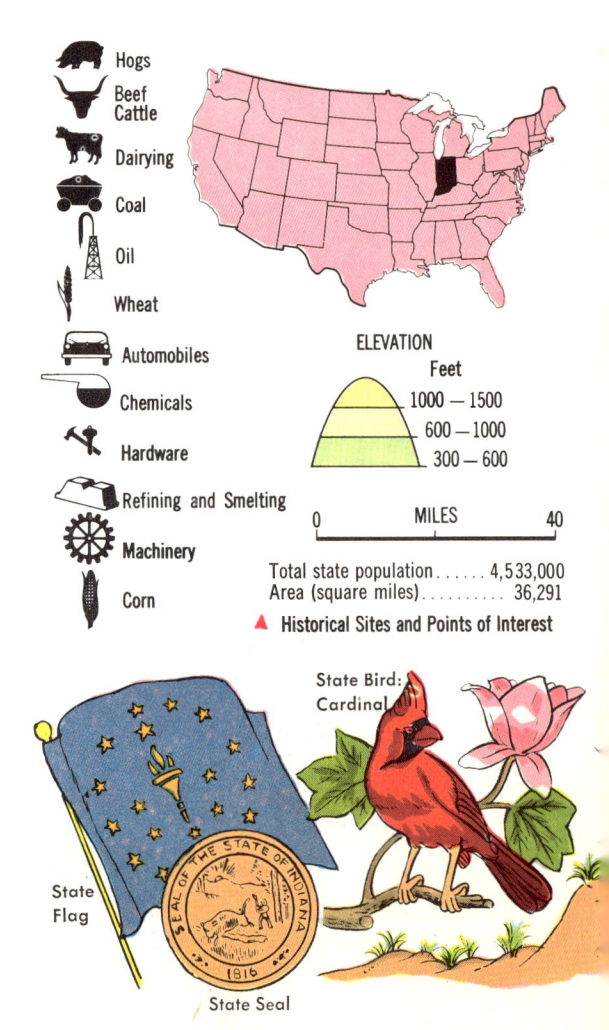

Hogs
Beef Cattle
Dairying
Coal
Oil
Wheat
Automobiles
Chemicals
Hardware
Refining and Smelting
Machinery
Corn

ELEVATION
Feet
1000 – 1500
600 – 1000
300 – 600

0   MILES   40

Total state population......4,533,000
Area (square miles).........36,291
▲ Historical Sites and Points of Interest

State Bird: Cardinal
State Flag
State Seal

INDIANA

699

LAKE MICHIGAN
MICHIGAN

East Chicago
Michigan City
Gary
Hammond
South Bend · Elkhart
Mishawaka
Steel-Producing Center

Fort Wayne

Wabash River

Site of Battle of Tippecanoe
Lafayette
Kokomo
Marion

Muncie
Anderson
Richmond

Motor Speedway
Indianapolis
Greenfield (Birthplace of James Whitcomb Riley)

Terre Haute

White River
Bloomington

West Fork
East Fork White River

Vincennes (First White Settlement in Indiana)

Wabash River

New Albany
Corydon (First State Capital, 1816)

Santa Claus
Evansville

Ohio River

ILLINOIS
OHIO
KENTUCKY

Tomato Canning
Mint for Mint Oil
Corn
Covered Bridge
Santa Claus Town
DEDICATED TO THE CHILDREN
and Dunes

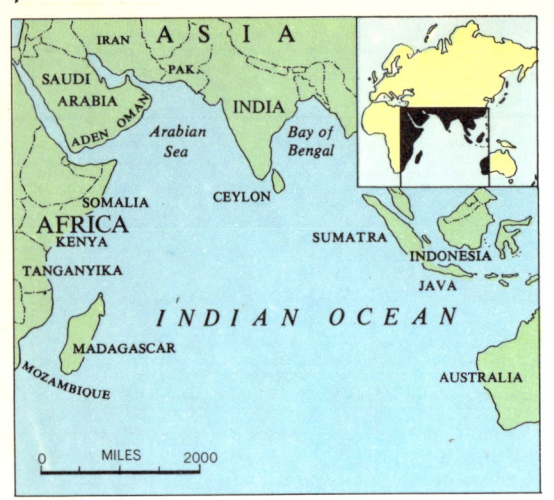

INDIAN OCEAN The Indian Ocean is the third-largest of our four oceans. It stretches all the way from Africa to the East Indies and Australia. Its waters wash the whole southern coast of the great continent of Asia. On the south it reaches to the continent of Antarctica. The land of India extends far out into this ocean. It gives the ocean its name.

For years the sailors of Europe were eager to reach India by sea. They wanted to bring back cargoes of spices and silk and perfume from India and the lands near by. At last they found a way around Africa into the Indian Ocean and on to India. But the voyage was long and hard.

Now there is a shorter way by sea from Europe to India and the Far East. This way goes through the Suez Canal. The Suez Canal joins the Mediterranean Sea and the Red Sea. The Mediterranean opens into the Atlantic. The Red Sea is an arm of the Indian Ocean.

There are many ways of going into the Indian Ocean from the Pacific. There are many passageways through the islands of the East Indies.

The Indian Ocean is warm. No wonder, for the equator crosses it. Sometimes there are hurricanes over the Indian Ocean, but as a rule the sea is calm. It is more pacific than the Pacific itself. (See EAST INDIES; INDIA; OCEANS; SUEZ CANAL.)

INDIAN PIPE The odd-looking Indian pipe is sometimes called "ghost flower." Both its stems and its flowers are white. It has no leaves. This plant has still another name—"corpse plant."

Indian pipe may be found in moist woods in many parts of the United States and in eastern Asia. But one has to watch the ground to see it. It almost never grows to be as much as a foot tall.

Since Indian pipe is white, it cannot make any food for itself. Only green plants can make their own food. Indian pipe gets its food mostly from dead leaves. Once in a while it gets its food from the roots of a living tree instead.

There are a great many kinds of plants that are white. But only a few of them have flowers. Strange as it may seem, Indian pipe is a relative of the beautiful trailing arbutus and the showy rhododendron.

It is easy to see how this plant got its name. It looks like the peace pipes many of the Indians used to smoke.

Some Indian pipe flowers are not as ghostlike as most of them are. Some have a faint pink color. Some even have red flowers. (See PLANT FACTORIES.)

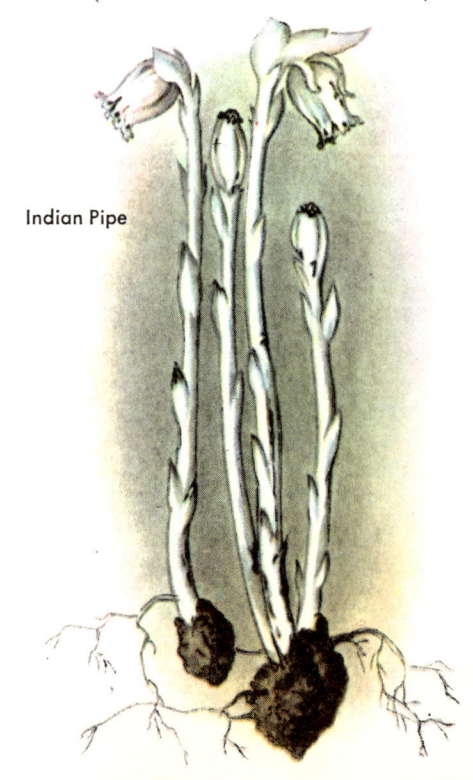

Indian Pipe

INDIANS, AMERICAN When Columbus landed in America he thought he had found India. He saw dark-skinned people with straight black hair and called them Indians. We still call these "first Americans" Indians today.

American Indians have nothing to do with India. But their ancestors, scientists think, did come from Asia. Long, long ago they crossed from Asia to what is now Alaska. They traveled southward and eastward. When the Spanish explorers who followed Columbus reached America, they found great Indian empires in Mexico and South America. There are still many Indians in the Americas. Some Indians even live in the barren lands at the very southern tip of South America.

There were hundreds of tribes of Indians in the area that became the United States. The many tribes can be divided into five groups. This list gives the groups and names a few of the tribes in each group:

Eastern tribes: Cherokee, Chippewa (or Ojibway), Choctaw, Cree, Creek, Delaware, Fox, Iroquois, Kickapoo, Miami, Mohican, Ottawa, Peoria, Potawatomi, Seminole, Shawnee, Winnebago.

Plains tribes: Arapaho, Blackfoot, Cheyenne, Comanche, Crow, Dakota (or Sioux), Kiowa, Missouri, Omaha, Osage, Pawnee, Paiute, Shoshone, Wichita.

Southwestern tribes: Apache, Hopi, Mohave, Navaho, Pima, Yuma, Zuñi.

California tribes: Maidu, Pomo, Witun.

Northwest coast tribes: Haida, Kwakiutl, Salish, Tlingit, Tsimshian, Yakima.

Even a person who does not know anything about Indians has heard some of these tribe names. For many are now the names of cities or rivers or states.

The Indians of different tribes had different kinds of homes. They had different languages and customs, too.

The eastern tribes are sometimes called Woodland Indians. They did some hunting with bows and arrows. They did much fishing. And they raised corn, beans, squash, and tobacco. Some of the tribes had learned to make their corn crops better by putting a dead fish in each hill of corn. The fish made good fertilizer. The farming was done by women, the hunting and fishing by men.

There are many rivers and streams in the East. The Indians traveled up and down them in canoes made of elm bark or birchbark or in dugouts made from logs.

The Iroquois Indians were five tribes joined together: the Mohawks, Oneidas, Onondagas, Cayugas, and Senecas. They are often called "The Five Nations." They all lived in upper New York state and southern Ontario.

The Iroquois were called "people of the longhouse." Many families lived together in long log houses covered with bark.

The homes of some of the eastern Indians were called wigwams. A wigwam was a small, round house made of poles and bark or hides. The homes of the Seminole Indians, who lived in the warm south, were called chickees. They had no walls.

The Indians of the Great Plains are often called buffalo Indians. The buffalo, or bison, furnished both meat and hides. Pictures of Indians riding ponies to hunt buffalo are common. But the Plains Indians hunted buffalo long before they had any horses. There were no horses in America until the early Spanish explorers brought some. Indian ponies descended from these Spanish horses.

The Plains Indians made clothing of soft buckskin. Some of it was decorated with fringe, porcupine quills, and elks' teeth. When trading with white people began, beads were used as decoration. Shoes were made of buckskin with tough buffalo-hide soles. The babies, or papooses, were wrapped in soft buckskins when they were put in their cradles. Thongs of buckskin held the babies in when their cradles were carried about on their mothers' backs.

The chiefs wore gorgeous feather headdresses. A chief wanted as many eagle feathers in his headdress as he could get. He thought the feathers would give him some of the eagle's strength and keen sight.

The Plains Indians did not farm. They kept moving from place to place to find good hunting. Their tepees, built of branches covered with skins, could easily be taken down and put up again. The Indians hauled their tepees from place to place on platforms fastened to two long poles. The French named this kind of wheelless cart a *travois* (tra VOY.)

The Indians of the Southwest had to fit their living to much heat and little water. Many of them lived in villages, or pueblos. Their homes were of sun-dried brick called adobe. Some were built one on top of another like apartment houses. Many pueblos were placed on cliffs for protection.

The Hopis were Pueblo Indians. They were good farmers. They made excellent pottery and wove beautiful baskets and cloth. Water was so scarce that they often tried to bring rain by magic. One of their ways was a snake dance. The dancers carried live rattlesnakes.

The Pueblo Indians were wise to build their houses where they could be protected, for some of the southwestern Indians were raiders and fighters. The Apaches and the Navaho were. They wandered about taking what they could. Later the Navaho gave up their wandering. They began raising big flocks of sheep. They learned to weave beautiful rugs and blankets. The Navahos learned, too, to make beautiful silver jewelry. They built homes called hogans.

The California Indians had a rather easy life. The climate was pleasant. They did not need to farm. Their chief food was acorns, and there were always plenty. They also ate wild berries and roots. Deer and rabbits furnished meat, but the Indians did little with the skins. Their clothing was made mostly of bark and grass.

The Indians of the Northwest were mostly fishermen. They were very skillful at spearing salmon. The great forests of the Northwest furnished wonderful logs for dugout canoes and for lodges. Beside their lodges stood tall, carved totem poles.

Some Indians were friendly to the white settlers. Some were not. As the settlers pushed westward, they had a great deal of trouble with unfriendly Indians. Of course, the Indians did not like the idea of being pushed out of their homes and their hunting grounds. There was often bloody fighting between the Indians and the settlers.

At last the United States Government set aside land for the Indians and forced them to live there. There are many Indian reservations west of the Mississippi. There are only a few in the East. Most of the eastern tribes have disappeared entirely. The Indians everywhere in the United States are citizens and have the right to vote. (See AZTECS; BISON; CLIFF DWELLERS; INCAS; MAYAS; TOTEM POLE.)

INDIANS

703

Arctic interior, Dene
Central woodland, Ojibway
Eastern woodland, Iroquois
Northwest coast, Tlingit
California, Pomo
Plains, Dakota
Southeast, Cherokee
Southwest, Navaho
Florida, Seminole
Pueblo, Hopi
Jungle, Jivaran
Amazon, Boro
Mexico, Huichol
Guatemala, Tzutuhil
Andes, Quechua
Antilles, Arawak
Andes, Aymara
Patagonia, Tehuelche
Plains, Toba
Mainland Arawak, Mojos
Brazilian highland, Botocudo
Coastal Fuegian

INDIANS OF THE AMERICAS

Native houses in Sumatra are built high above the ground.

Divers search for pearl oysters off the islands.

INDIAN SUMMER Almost every year in most of the United States there are bright, summery days late in the fall. These days are called Indian summer.

Canada and northern Europe have an Indian summer, too. In Europe it used to be called "St. Martin's summer," or "Old Woman's summer." But now, in parts of Europe, it is called Indian summer just as it is in the United States.

No one knows how the name came about. One guess is that the Indians told the Pilgrims that there would be another short summer after harvest time. But the name is not found in books for nearly 200 years after the Pilgrims landed.

Every year on one Sunday at Indian summer time a Chicago newspaper prints the same cartoon. It shows a small boy looking out at a cornfield at dusk. The corn is in shocks. The little boy as he watches thinks he sees the ghosts of Indians dancing about their campfires. He imagines that the corn shocks are tepees. The rustling of the leaves is made by the dancing.

INDONESIA After World War II several new nations were born. One of them was Indonesia.

Indonesia is made up of many islands, some of them very large. For a long period before 1949 all the islands that are now Indonesia were parts of the Netherlands Indies. They were under the rule of the Dutch. Now the people of Indonesia rule themselves. The nation is a republic.

The map shows all the larger islands of Indonesia. In all the islands together there is a little more land than there is in Alaska. But Indonesia has 400 times as many people as there are in Alaska. Much land in the islands is mountainous. More than 100 of the mountains are volcanoes. Dense jungle, in which few people live, covers parts of the islands. It is easy to see, then, that some parts of Indonesia must be very crowded. They are. The lowlands in Java make up one of the most crowded regions in the whole world.

Indonesia can furnish a living for a great many people. In spite of the moun-

INDONESIA

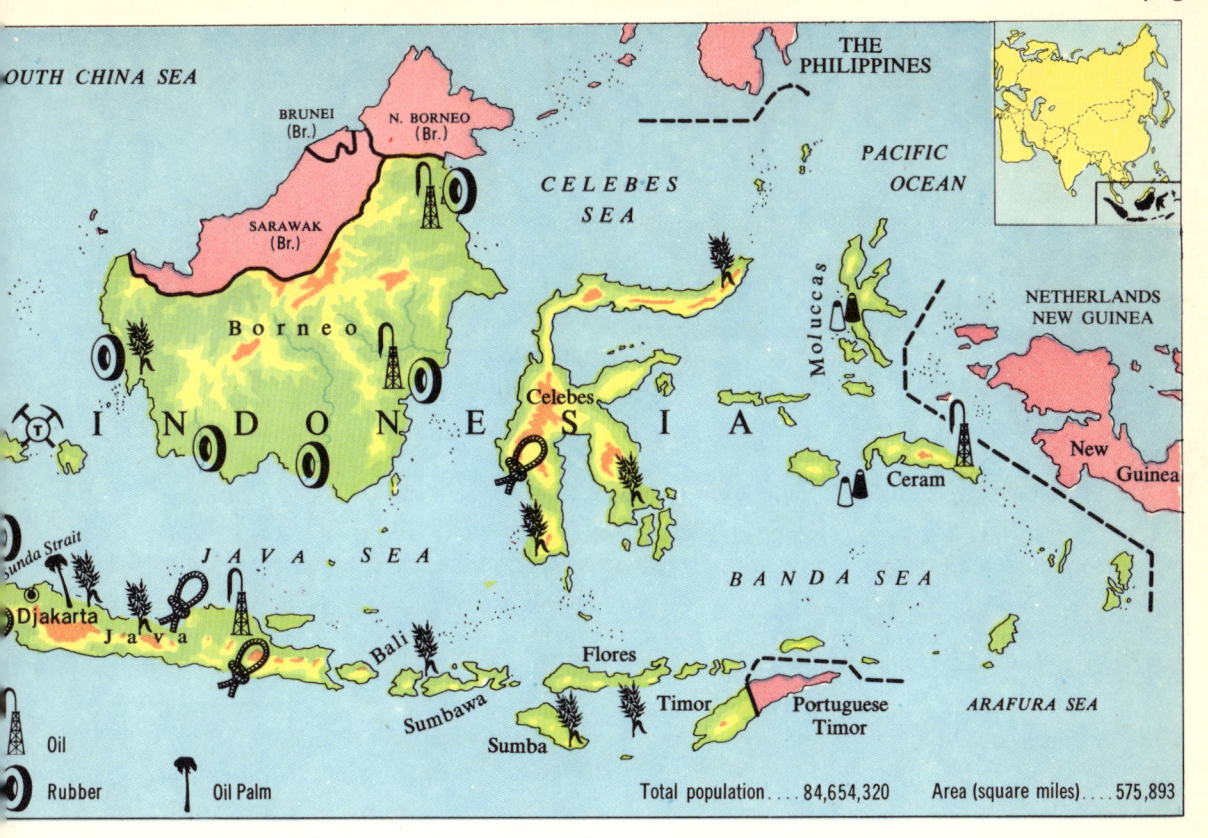

tains and jungles there is much good crop land. Now more than two-thirds of the people of the islands are farmers living in small villages. The soil is fertile. There is much rainfall and warmth. The equator crosses Indonesia, and all days there are hot. In some months there is much more rain than in others. People from cooler lands find the hot, rainy months hard to bear, but the heat and rain make it possible to raise crops the year round. Any month may be a harvest month.

Many voyages in the time of Columbus were attempts to find a new route to these islands to get spices. Today, rice, rubber, tea, coffee, palm oil, and quinine are more important exports than spices.

The islands are rich in tin and in oil. There are other minerals, too. Tin, oil, and some teakwood from the forests are exported. New roads are being built. More and more places far apart in the islands are being linked by Indonesian air lines. Many people work in shipyards, oil refineries, and textile, paper, tire, and other factories. More and more young Indonesians are being trained to plan and manage factories and transport lines.

In the islands there is a great mixture of races and languages. Some recent disputes there were serious. Indonesia's success will depend partly on how well its people work together. (See EAST INDIES.)

Indonesia has great plantations.

Factory towns were rows of tiny, dark houses.

INDUSTRIAL REVOLUTION For many, many centuries most of the work of the world was done by hand. Men had tools, but they used their own muscles in working with them. Some two centuries ago a great change began. Machines began to take the place of workmen. This period of change is called the Industrial Revolution.

The revolution started in England. It began with the spinning and weaving industry. Just before 1770 the spinning of yarn and the weaving of cloth were done in almost the same way in which they had been done for 3,000 years. In 1770 the spinning jenny was invented. With it one man could do the work of eight people.

Soon there were better spinning machines. Some were run by water power. Before long there were looms run by water power. Then came the steam engine. A steam engine of a kind had been invented nearly 2,000 years earlier. But now James Watt invented one that could run other machines. The machines for spinning and weaving no longer had to be near streams. Steam engines could be used anywhere.

The use of machines spread to other industries. It spread to other countries.

At first thought it would seem that everyone would be glad to have work made easy. But the coming of the machines put many men out of work. If one man with a big machine could do the work of 100 men, 99 men had to find some other way of earning a living. There were riots, and the workmen tried to destroy the machines that were taking their jobs away.

Before the coming of the machine, many workers did their work at home. But big machines run by water power or steam engines could not be put in people's homes. Factories grew up. Tenement houses were built near the factories. The workers were crowded into these tenements.

Another bad effect of the coming of the machine was the hiring of children as factory workers. Children could be paid less than grown people. It came to be common for children to work in factories for 12 to 14 hours a day. Many of these children were badly treated besides.

When a man worked in his own way, he was likely to take pride in his work. When he worked a machine, he could not follow his own ideas. Here was another bad effect of the coming of the machine.

Coal became important in the Industrial Revolution.

Women, and even children, worked in factories.

There was, too, the danger of getting hurt with the machines. There was much more danger than with hand tools.

Some of these bad effects did not have to be. Much has been done to right them. There are now, for example, child labor laws that keep children from working in factories. There are laws that protect adult workers, too. Factory work today is very different from work in early factories.

There were, of course, great benefits from the Industrial Revolution. The machines meant the end of much back-breaking work. Manufactured goods, moreover, could be made much more cheaply and in much larger amounts than before. Things that only kings and queens could have in earlier times could be bought by almost anyone. And many of our comforts of today would not be possible at all without machines. We could not, for instance, have electric lights if there were no big electric generators. No one would want to go back to the days before the Industrial Revolution. (See ENGINES; FACTORIES; INVENTIONS; LABOR UNIONS; MACHINERY; SPINNING AND WEAVING.)

INDUSTRIES Some countries are chiefly farming countries. Most of their people make a living by working on the land. Other countries are industrial countries. Many of their people make a living by working in factories, mines, and mills. Much of their work is done with big machines.

The United States is an industrial country. It has wonderful farms, but there are not nearly as many farmers as there are other workers in industry. Only about a tenth of the working people are farmers.

The United States can boast of a great many different industries. The pictures on the right show some of the most important. These industries together give work to many millions of people. (See FACTORIES; IRON AND STEEL; LUMBERING; MINES AND MINING; NATURAL GAS; PETROLEUM; PRINTING.)

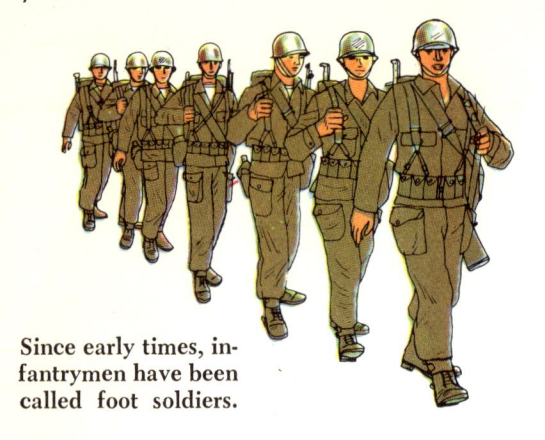

Since early times, infantrymen have been called foot soldiers.

INFANTRY Ever since there have been organized armies, there have been infantry soldiers. Infantrymen are foot soldiers. Throughout the many wars of history, they have been in the thick of the fighting.

Infantry soldiers carry their own weapons, ammunition, food, and other supplies. For centuries they have marched into battle. In modern times they have often been carried to the scene of action in trucks or planes. Most infantrymen in World War II, however, had to move on foot as soldiers have done for centuries.

Foot soldiers must keep in good physical condition. They must be able to march many miles carrying many pounds of equipment. They must be able to live out of doors in all kinds of weather.

Often in the past it has been said that the newest weapons would do away with the need for infantry soldiers in war. This was said when gunpowder was developed. It was said again when airplanes were developed, and again when the atom bomb came into use. But every nation that has an army still trains most of its men as foot soldiers. (See U. S. ARMED FORCES.)

INFLUENZA At the end of World War I an epidemic swept over Europe and the United States, killing a tremendous number of people. The disease was influenza, or "flu." Influenza usually is not a dangerous disease. It is, however, rather tricky. People who have influenza often think that they are over it and get out of bed too soon. Then, a few days later, they get sick again and have to go back to bed.

A person with flu usually has chills and fever. He is likely to ache all over.

Scientists had a hard time finding out what causes influenza. Now they have found that it is caused by a virus. A person can have the disease again and again. But vaccines have been developed that help keep people from having it. (See DISEASE GERMS; DISEASES.)

INFRARED RAYS Ordinary sunlight has in it the many colors that we see in a rainbow. They all come to us from the sun in rays. The sun also sends out many rays which we cannot see. Some of these invisible rays are called infrared radiation.

Infrared rays are given off by anything that is hot. By using special film, it is possible to take a picture of a hot electric iron in a darkened room. Infrared rays are a great help in aerial photography. They can pass through clouds and mist better than visible light rays. Infrared cameras are also used for taking pictures of the distant stars.

Infrared rays produce heat when they strike any kind of matter. Some of the warmth we feel from the sun comes from visible light rays, but much of it comes from the infrared radiation. Doctors use infrared rays to produce heat in certain medical treatments. Foods that are broiled are chiefly cooked by infrared rays.

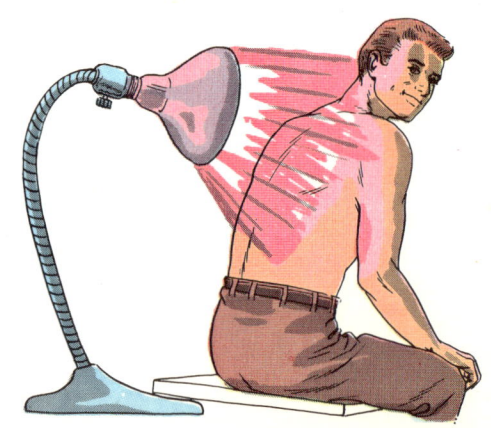

Infrared rays help in medical treatments.

INK

INK More than 4,000 years ago the Egyptians were writing with ink on papyrus. Ink is older than paper. The ink of the Egyptians was made of powdered charcoal and some kind of glue. It could be wiped off with a sponge. Sometimes, if an Egyptian writer made a mistake, he licked off the ink with his tongue. The Romans, centuries later, were still using the same kind of ink. An old story tells that one Roman emperor used to make poets lick off any of their poems he did not like.

The Romans used another kind of ink, too. They got this ink from an animal in the sea—the squid. When a squid is disturbed it sends out a dark-brown liquid to make a kind of smoke screen around itself. The Romans found that they could write with this brown fluid. We call it sepia.

About 1,000 years ago a new kind of ink was invented. It was made from galls from oak trees. Oak galls are woody lumps that grow around the eggs that gall insects lay in oak twigs. There is tannin in these galls. When certain chemicals are added to the tannin, excellent ink is made. During the Middle Ages every writer had his own recipe for ink. Much of the writing done then is as clear today as if it had just been done.

Today there are many kinds of ink. There is ink of every color. Aniline dyes have made all these colors possible. Some ink is made especially for fountain pens. Some is made for ball-point pens. Some is used only in printing. Artists use India ink, which is not good for ordinary writing or printing. Many different materials are used in the many kinds of ink.

There are even many kinds of invisible ink. Sometimes secret messages are written in them. The messages do not show until the writing is treated in some way. Probably the simplest kind of invisible ink is lemon juice. The writing done with it does not show until it is heated. Then the lemon juice scorches and the writing turns brown and is visible. (See DYES; GALLS; SECRET WRITING; SQUIDS; WRITING.)

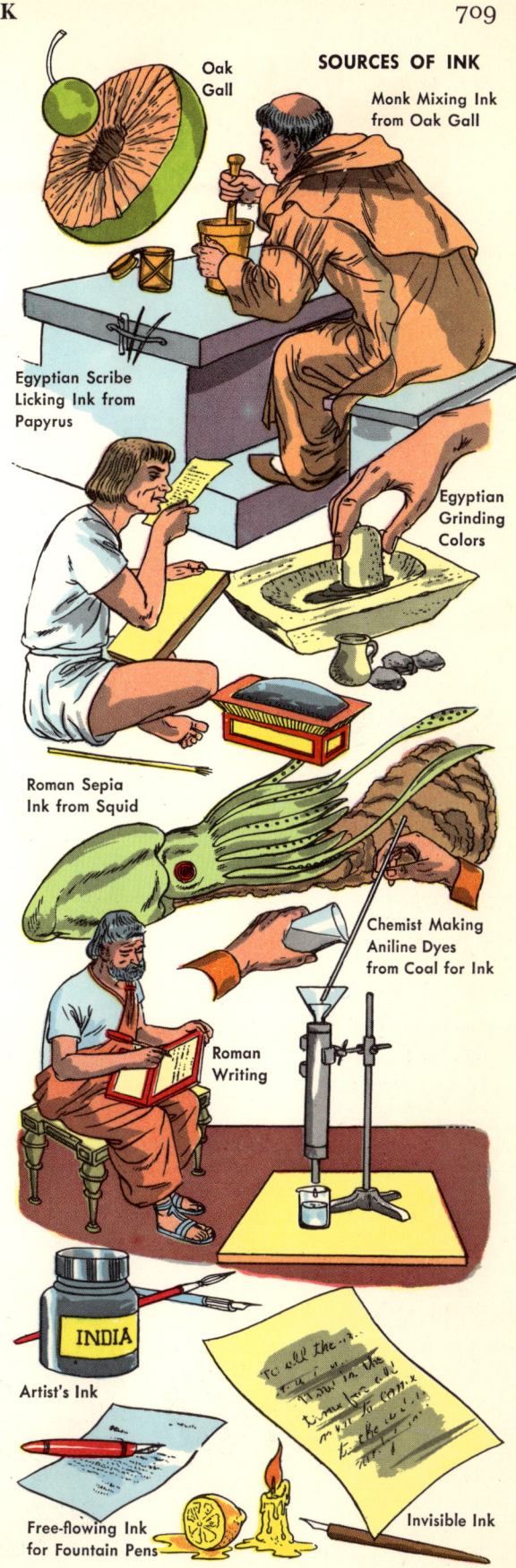

SOURCES OF INK

Oak Gall

Monk Mixing Ink from Oak Gall

Egyptian Scribe Licking Ink from Papyrus

Egyptian Grinding Colors

Roman Sepia Ink from Squid

Chemist Making Aniline Dyes from Coal for Ink

Roman Writing

Artist's Ink

Free-flowing Ink for Fountain Pens

Invisible Ink

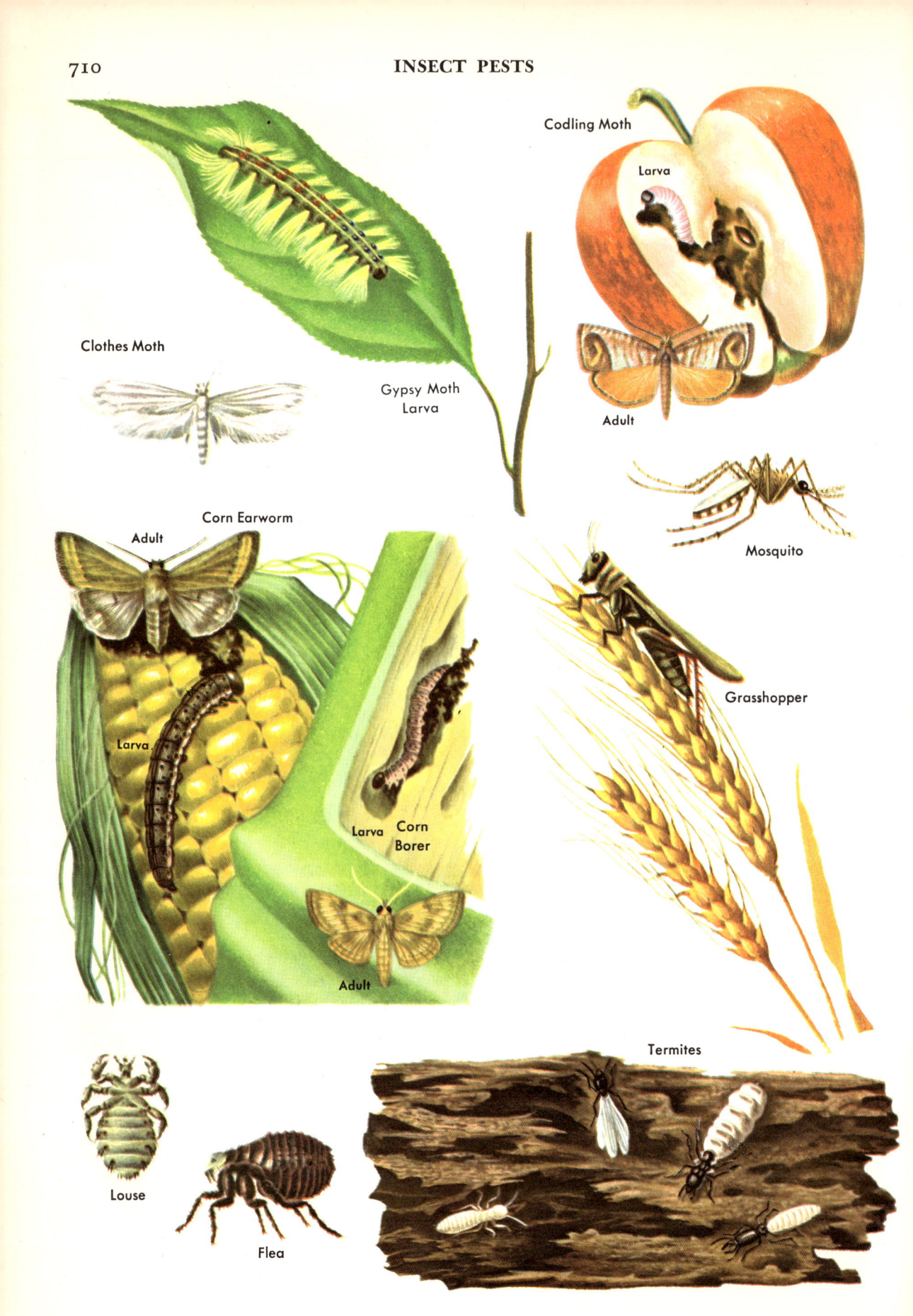

INSECT PESTS

INSECT PESTS

INSECT PESTS Once the reptiles were the lords of the earth. But in time most of them were crowded out by other animals. People are the lords of the earth now. Will they, too, be crowded out?

The only real rivals we have are the insects. There are more than half a million kinds. And there are a great many of each kind. Probably there are about half a million insects to every one person. We run a race with insects for much of our food. Insects injure our houses and clothing. They do great damage to our forest and shade trees. Worst of all, they carry diseases. Is there any chance that they will crowd people off the earth? Probably not. But we shall always have to fight them.

Not all insects are harmful pests. Some are true helpers. Some even help us in fighting harmful insects.

The insects that harm us are called insect pests. The pictures show several of these harmful insects.

The housefly is one of the disease carriers. It carries typhoid fever. One kind of mosquito carries malaria. Another kind carries yellow fever. Fleas carry a terrible disease called bubonic plague. The louse carries typhus.

The clothes moth costs the people of the United States over $20,000,000 a year. This moth, when it is a caterpillar, eats holes in woolen clothes and rugs. It ruins furs. Cockroaches get into food. Silverfish ruin books. Ants and larder beetles are among the other insects that are great nuisances in our houses. Termites may destroy the wood of the houses themselves.

Many insects harm our garden plants. The potato beetle, the corn earworm, and the cabbage butterfly are three of them.

Our fruit trees also have many enemies. The codling moth spoils many apples. The peach borer harms peach trees. The cottony cushion scale attacks orange trees.

The gypsy moth is an enemy of forest and shade trees. No part of a tree is safe from insects. Some eat the leaves, some suck the sap, some bore into the wood. Some injure the roots, buds, or young twigs.

Millions of dollars' worth of damage is done to our fields of corn each year by the corn borer. The chinch bug and the boll weevil are "million dollar" insect pests, too. The boll weevil ruins much cotton, the chinch bug much wheat. At times grasshoppers do great damage to crops.

There are several ways to fight our insect enemies. One way is to catch them in traps of some kind. Another is to encourage birds and other animals that eat insects. Other ways are to use chemicals to kill insects and to destroy insect breeding places. By using all these ways we should be able to hold our own against our insect rivals. (See BEETLES; BUGS; DISEASES; INSECTS; MOSQUITO.)

Silverfish and bedbugs are two common household insect pests. Both insects are wingless.

INSECTS

Aedes Mosquito

Cecropia Moth

Locusts

Walkingstick

Tailed Blue

American Copper

Buffalo Carpet Beetle

Duck Louse

Ladybirds

Yellow Jacket

Housefly

INSECTS

Order	Common Name
THYSANURA	Silverfish
PLECOPTERA	Stoneflies
ODONATA	Dragonflies
ORTHOPTERA	Grasshoppers
EPHEMEROPTERA	Mayflies
CORRODENTIA	Book Lice
TRICHOPTERA	Caddisflies
ISOPTERA	Termites
MALLOPHAGA	Chewing Lice
ANOPLURA	Sucking Lice
HOMOPTERA	Aphids, Scales
HEMIPTERA	True Bugs
NEUROPTERA	Aphid-Lion
SIPHONAPTERA	Fleas
DIPTERA	Flies
COLEOPTERA	Beetles
HYMENOPTERA	Wasps, Bees
LEPIDOPTERA	Moths and Butterflies

INSECTS Suppose a list were made of all the kinds of insects in the world. And suppose the list were printed on a long strip of paper in type like this, with only one name on a line. The strip of paper would have to be nearly two miles long! For there are more than half a million kinds of insects. The kinds of insects outnumber the kinds of all other animals put together.

Insects live in almost every kind of place. There are not many in the sea, but they are found almost everywhere in fresh water and on land. Most mountaintops are not too high and most hot springs are not too hot for them. Even in Antarctica a few kinds of insects have been found.

Another name for insects is "hexapods." This name means "six-footed." All insects have six legs. They are all alike in other ways, too. They all have one pair of feelers. They all are covered with a remarkable waterproof substance called chitin. Their bodies are divided into three parts: the head, the thorax, and the abdomen.

Most insects, but not quite all, have two big eyes made up of many little ones. Eyes of this kind are called compound eyes.

One may see insects crawling, hopping, swimming, jumping, or walking, but flying is the usual insect way of getting about. Most insects have wings. Some can fly very fast for a short distance. The dragonfly is one of the fast fliers.

As a rule insects are air-breathers. Branching tubes carry air to all parts of their bodies. Air gets into these tubes through tiny holes called spiracles.

It is easy to tell an insect from other animals. But no one should think that all insects are almost alike. There are many differences between different insects. Some insects have two pairs of wings. Some have one pair. Some have none at all. Insects differ from one another in shape. Ladybirds, walking sticks, and butterflies are certainly not shaped much alike. Different insects have different kinds of mouths for eating different kinds of food. Leaves, blood, nectar, plant sap, wool, wood, and other insects are all insect food. And insects differ, too, in size and color.

Some insects go through four stages as they grow up. A butterfly is first an egg. The egg hatches into a caterpillar, or larva. The caterpillar grows, sheds its skin several times, and at last forms a case around itself. It is now called a pupa. The pupa changes to a grown-up butterfly.

A grasshopper, on the other hand, is never a caterpillar. When it hatches from an egg it looks like a grown-up grasshopper except that it does not have wings. It grows, sheds its skin several times, grows wings, and finally reaches its full size.

Many insects follow the butterfly plan of growing up. Most of the rest follow the grasshopper plan.

Scientists have grouped the hundreds of thousands of kinds of insects into big groups called orders. The chart on the opposite page shows the chief orders. The scientists' names for many of these orders end in "ptera." "Ptera" comes from the Greek and means "wings." Moths and butterflies are *Lepidoptera.* "*Lepidoptera*" means "scaly wings." Flies and mosquitoes are *Diptera.* "*Diptera*" means "two wings."

Insects of some kinds live together in big insect cities, or societies. They help one another. They divide up the jobs to be done. They seem to get along together better than people often do. The history of some of these insects has been millions of years longer than that of people. (See ANTS; BEE; BEETLES; BUGS; BUTTERFLIES AND MOTHS; LARVA; MOSQUITO; TERMITES; WASPS.)

PARTS OF AN INSECT

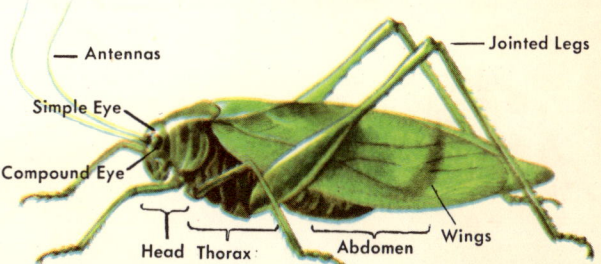

INSURANCE

Insurance companies will pay for the damage caused by many kinds of disasters.

INSURANCE Mr. Brown builds a house. As soon as his house is built there is a chance that it will catch on fire. It may burn to the ground. Mr. Brown runs the risk of losing all that he put into it. But he can pay to have someone else share the risk. He can get a company to agree, in case the house burns down, to pay him most of what the house was worth before the fire.

Making this kind of arrangement is called insuring a house against fire. The written arrangement is called a fire insurance policy. The company that makes the arrangement is called a fire insurance company. Mr. Brown pays a small amount of money each year to the insurance company for the policy.

Of course, if most houses burned down, no company could afford to insure houses. But most houses do not burn down. Suppose the owners of 100,000 houses have fire insurance with one company. Suppose, too, that 1,000 of these owners have fires that damage their houses. The company pays for the damage done. It does not have to pay anything to the other 99,000 owners. The money they have paid in makes it possible for the company to pay for the houses that burned. But the 99,000 owners get something for the money they paid in. They are saved a great deal of worry.

There are many different kinds of insurance. There is some kind of insurance to protect us against almost every kind of misfortune. Here are some of the many kinds of insurance that Mr. Brown might carry besides fire insurance.

Wind and tornado insurance — Mr. Brown can insure his house and any other buildings he owns against windstorms.

Accident insurance — Mr. Brown can insure himself against accidents. If he has an accident, his insurance will help him pay his doctor bills. It may pay all of them. If the accident does him some permanent harm, his insurance will pay him something to make up for this harm.

Health insurance — Many people lose their wages if they are sick. Mr. Brown can buy health insurance that will give him money to live on while he cannot earn any.

Life insurance — Mr. Brown, let us suppose, has a wife and three children. If he has life insurance, he does not have to worry for fear his family will have nothing to live on if he should die. If he dies, the life insurance company will pay them the amount he has arranged for.

Automobile liability insurance—If Mr. Brown owns a car, he should certainly own liability insurance. The insurance company will pay for the damage if his car damages another car in an accident.

Theft insurance—Mr. Brown can insure his car, the furniture in his house, his jewelry, and other such valuable possessions against being stolen. Of course, they may be stolen anyway, but if they are, Mr. Brown will get a large part of what they are worth from the insurance company.

Many people have all the kinds of insurance listed above. There are other kinds of insurance that not so many people have. Only farmers, for instance, have crop insurance. Crop insurance saves them from worrying for fear their crops will be ruined by storms or by insects. There is special insurance for shippers, too. It protects goods that are being shipped. Even special events like carnivals can be insured. Such an event may cost a great deal of money. If a carnival is insured, for instance, some of the money it cost can be recovered if bad weather ruins the celebration.

The money that a person pays to the insurance company is called a premium. Premiums for the same kind of insurance may differ a great deal. Fire insurance premiums are lower in a city that has a good fire department than they are in a village with no fire department. Life insurance premiums are lower for young people than for old people. Where the risk is less, insurance premiums are less.

The United States has many big insurance companies. Americans spend more on insurance than do the people of any other country. One city—Hartford, Conn.—is known as the "Insurance Capital of the World." But the most famous insurance company is not an American company. It is an English company—Lloyd's of London. Lloyd's deals mainly in marine, or ship insurance, but it will insure almost anything considered a fair risk. It has even insured pianists' fingers and dancers' feet.

Through reading a child learns many new things.

INTELLIGENCE QUOTIENT Some people are able to understand quickly and remember for a long time what they hear, see, and read. They are able to use facts and ideas in a skillful way. When they meet a problem, they are able to think how to solve it. These people are said to be very intelligent. Other people who are less able to do these things are, of course, considered to be less intelligent.

Scientists have found out how well the average person thinks and acts at each age. They have learned what to expect of a 2-year-old, a 3-year-old, and so on. They have worked out tests to show how well a person can do what is expected of him. The tests may show that a 10-year-old can do what is expected of a 14-year-old. He then is very intelligent. His I.Q., or intelligence quotient, is said to be 140. If he can do just what is expected of a 10-year-old, his I.Q., or intelligence quotient, is 100. The score of 100 means the child is average for his age. If he does only what is expected of an 8-year-old, his I.Q. is 80.

The first step in finding a person's I.Q. is to find out his mental age by giving him an intelligence test. His mental age is next multiplied by 100. The result is then divided by his actual age. The answer is his intelligence quotient.

$$\frac{\text{Mental Age} \times 100}{\text{Age in Years}} = \text{I.Q.}$$

$$\frac{14 \text{ (Mental Age)} \times 100}{10 \text{ (Age in Years)}} = 140 \text{ (I.Q.)}$$

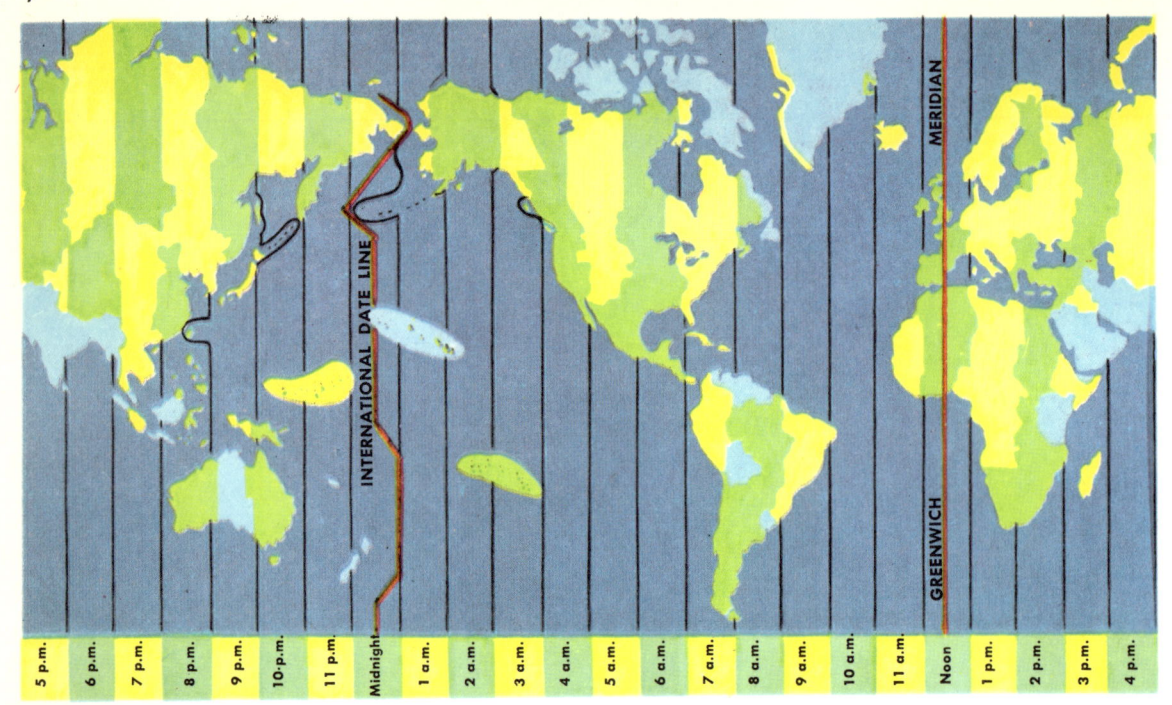

INTERNATIONAL DATE LINE Between Alaska and Siberia there are two islands called the Diomedes. One is Big Diomede. The other is Little Diomede. These two islands are only two miles apart. But a strange thing happens to anyone who goes from one island to the other. He goes to another day in the week!

If he goes from Big Diomede to Little Diomede he goes back to the day before. If he goes from Little Diomede to Big Diomede he jumps to the day ahead. The reason this strange thing happens is that the imaginary line called the International Date Line goes between these two islands.

It is never the same time everywhere in the world. When it is six o'clock in the evening in New York, it is only three o'clock in San Francisco. But it is midnight in London. "Later east, earlier west" is a good rule in thinking of time. But there must be a starting place. The starting place is the International Date Line.

Little Diomede is just barely east of the International Date Line. Big Diomede is just barely west of it. Suppose it is Tuesday noon on Little Diomede. There are 24 hours in a day. Every 24th of the way around the world makes an hour's difference in time. In London, halfway around the world, it is midnight on Tuesday. Halfway on around the world at Big Diomede, it is 12 hours later still. It is noon on Wednesday. So moving from one Diomede to the other means going to another day of the week.

The International Date Line runs all the way from the North Pole to the South Pole. For most of the way it is in the middle of the Pacific Ocean.

One of the ships of the explorer Magellan was the first ship to sail around the world. It took almost three years to make the journey. The sailors kept track of time carefully. The day they landed they were sure was Wednesday. But it turned out to be Thursday instead. They did not understand how they had lost a day. Of course, they had sailed west across the International Date Line.

Edgar Allan Poe once wrote a story called "Three Sundays in a Week." You could not get three whole Sundays in a week, but you could get three in eight days by sailing over the International Date Line and back. (See LATITUDE AND LONGITUDE; TIME AND TIME TELLING.)

INVENTIONS

INVENTIONS Almost everything we have or use had to be invented. Doorbells, telephones, stoves, lamps, refrigerators, printing presses, farm machinery, tools, dynamite, glass, steel—this is only the beginning of a list that could be made many pages long. Of course, air and water and grass and trees did not have to be invented. But inventions fan air into our buildings, pump water to where it is needed, and help in planting grass and trees and taking care of them. Food did not have to be invented, either. But our cave-men ancestors would probably have starved to death if they had not invented weapons for killing wild animals to eat. And certainly the land of the world could not possibly produce enough food for all the millions of people on it now if machines had not been invented for tilling the soil.

Some very important inventions were made long before any records were kept—long before anyone knew how to write. The knife, the spear, the bow and arrow, ways of making fire, and ways of making cloth and pottery are a few of them. No one has any idea who the inventors of these things were. Even with modern inventions it is not always easy to name the inventor. One person puts on the final touch, but his work is based on the work of many others. It is not possible, for instance, to name one inventor for the automobile. Early automobiles were developed by putting together many inventions.

In some cases two inventors have invented almost the same thing at almost the same time, even though neither one knew anything about the work of the other. There is an old saying, "Necessity is the mother of invention." It is a good saying. When there is a need for some new device, many people work on it and sooner or later one of them has an idea that turns out to be good. Perhaps more than one person may have the same idea at almost the same time.

Almost every invention is promptly improved. Edison invented the electric light bulb. But those we use now are not much like Edison's invention. Bell invented the telephone. But many people, if they could see his first telephone, would not know what it was.

The list on the next page names some of the great inventions of modern times. It names the person who is given credit for the invention. It also tells where and when the invention was made. (See PATENTS.)

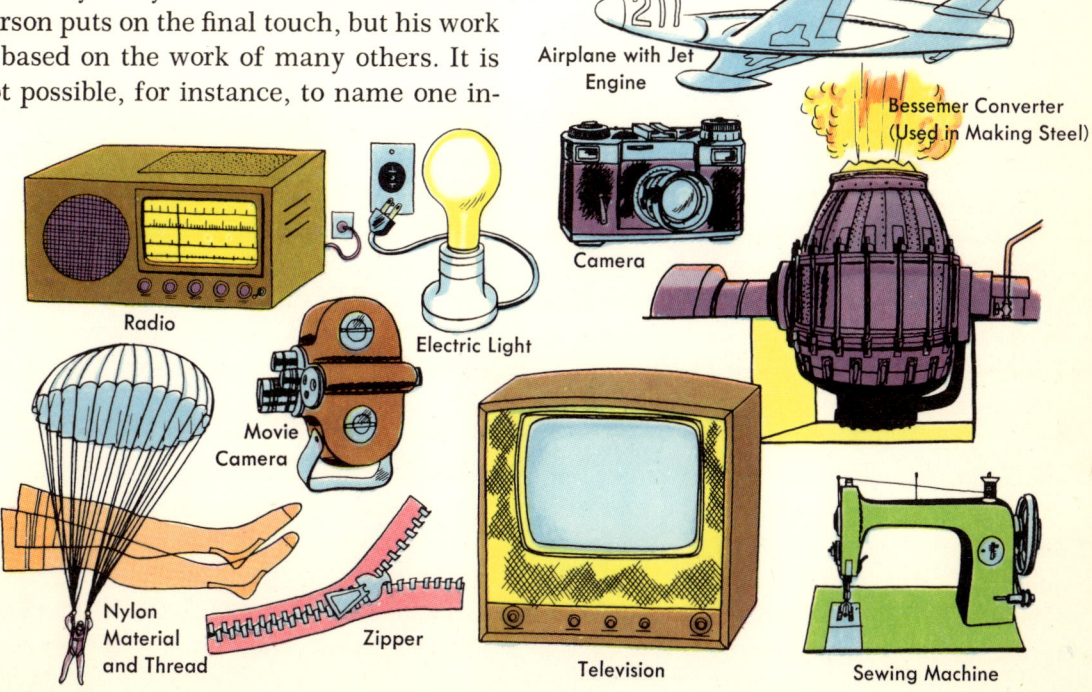

INVENTIONS

Airplane with Jet Engine

Bessemer Converter (Used in Making Steel)

Radio

Camera

Electric Light

Movie Camera

Nylon Material and Thread

Zipper

Television

Sewing Machine

INVENTIONS

INVENTION	INVENTOR	COUNTRY	DATE
Air brake	George Westinghouse	United States	1868
Air conditioning	W. H. Carrier	United States	1911
Airplane	Wilbur and Orville Wright	United States	1903
Barometer	Evangelista Torricelli	Italy	1643
Bessemer converter	Sir Henry Bessemer	England	1856
Bicycle	Kirkpatrick MacMillan	Scotland	1839
Canning	François Appert	France	1804
Cash register	James Ritty	United States	1879
Celluloid	John W. Hyatt	United States	1869
CinemaScope	Henri Chretien	France	1931
Clock, pendulum	Christian Huygens	Netherlands	1656
Cotton gin	Eli Whitney	United States	1793
Cyclotron	Ernest O. Lawrence	United States	1931
Diesel engine	Rudolf Diesel	Germany	1892
Dynamite	Alfred Nobel	Sweden	1862
Electromagnet	William Sturgeon	England	1825
Electric lamp bulb	Thomas Edison	United States	1879
Electric generator	Michael Faraday	England	1831
Electric motor, A.C.	Nikola Tesla	United States	1892
Electric trolley	Frank J. Sprague	United States	1887
Elevator, passenger	Elisha G. Otis	United States	1861
Fountain pen	Lewis E. Waterman	United States	1884
Gyrocompass	Elmer A. Sperry	United States	1911
Gyroscope	Léon Foucault	France	1852
Hydroplane	Glenn H. Curtiss	United States	1911
Internal combustion engine	Gottlieb Daimler	Germany	1885
Jet propulsion	Sir Frank Whittle	England	1930
Kodak	George Eastman	United States	1888
Linotype machine	Ottmar Mergenthaler	United States	1885
Locomotive, steam	Richard Trevithick	England	1804
Machine gun	Richard J. Gatling	United States	1861
Match, friction	John Walker	England	1827
Microscope, compound	Zacharias Janssen	Netherlands	1590
Movie projector	Thomas Edison	United States	1893
Nylon	W. H. Carothers	United States	1930

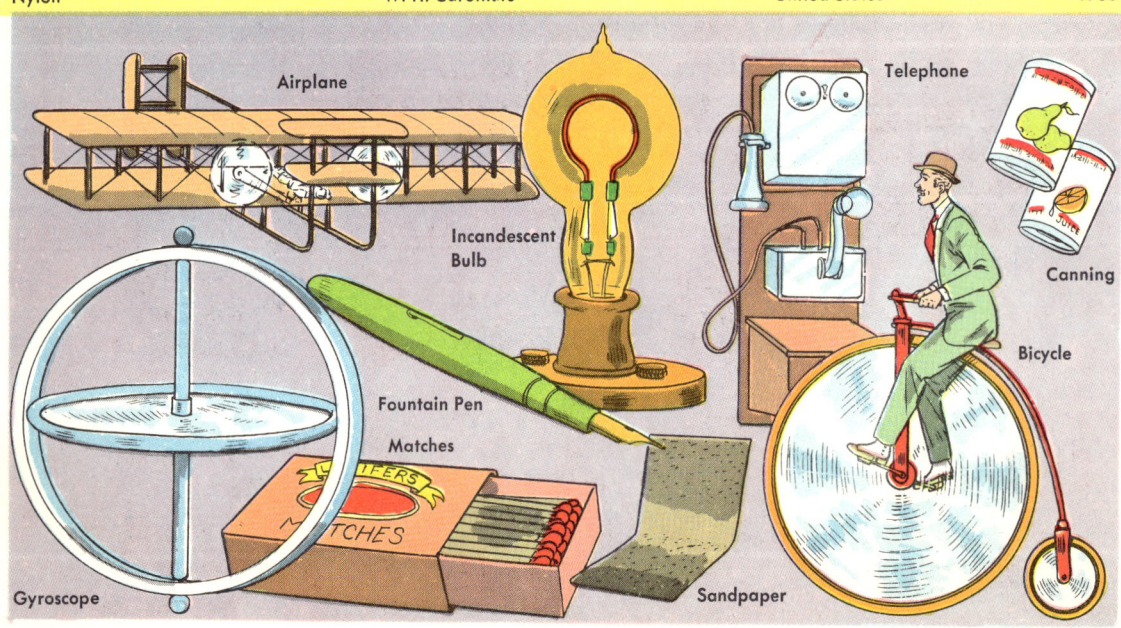

INVENTIONS

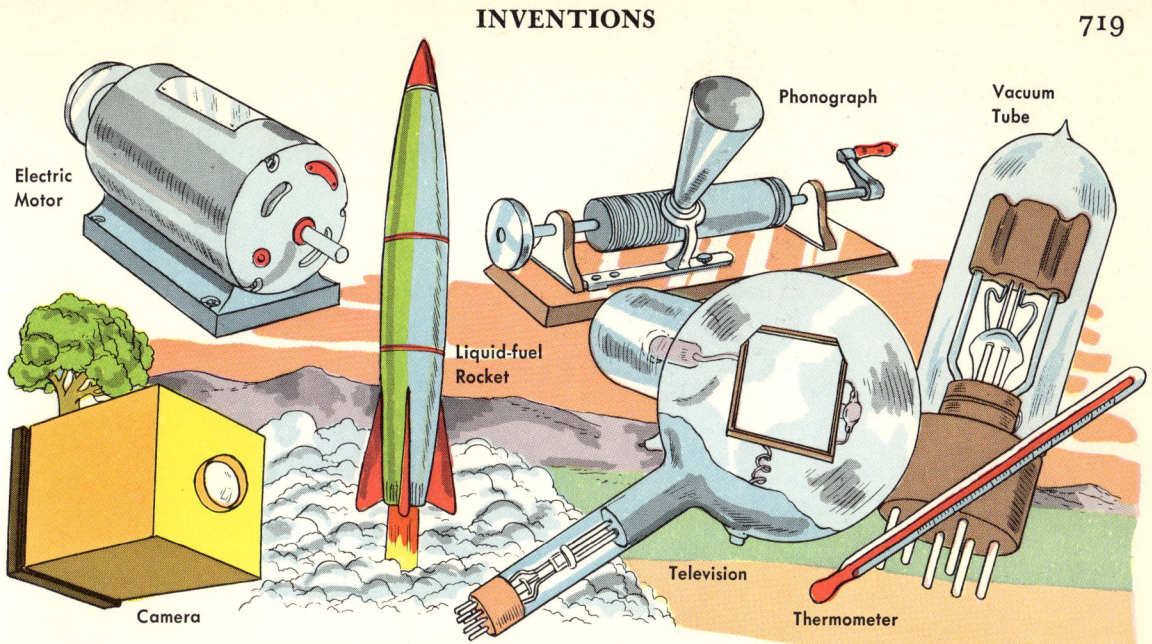

719

Electric Motor
Liquid-fuel Rocket
Phonograph
Vacuum Tube
Camera
Television
Thermometer

INVENTION	INVENTOR	COUNTRY	DATE
Papermaking machine	Louis Robert	France	1798
Parachute	François Blanchard	France	1785
Phonograph	Thomas Edison	United States	1877
Photography, black and white	Louis Daguerre	France	1839
Photography, color	Gabriel Lippman	France	1891
Pneumatic tire	John B. Dunlop	North Ireland	1888
Printing press	Johann Gutenberg (?)	Germany	1450
Quick freezing of food	Clarence Birdseye	United States	1925
Radio	Guglielmo Marconi	Italy	1895
Reaper	Cyrus McCormick	United States	1834
Refrigeration, mechanical	Jacob Perkins	United States	1834
Rifle, automatic	John M. Browning	United States	1918
Rocket, liquid fuel	Robert H. Goddard	United States	1926
Rubber, vulcanized	Charles Goodyear	United States	1839
Safety lamp	Sir Humphry Davy	England	1816
Safety pin	Walter Hunt	United States	1849
Sewing machine	Elias Howe	United States	1846
Sleeping car	George M. Pullman	United States	1858
Spinning jenny	James Hargreaves	England	1764
Steam engine	James Watt	Scotland	1765
Steamboat	Robert Fulton	United States	1807
Submarine	John P. Holland	United States	1891
Tank, Military	Sir Ernest Swinton	England	1914
Telegraph	Samuel F. B. Morse	United States	1837
Telephone	Alexander Graham Bell	United States	1876
Telescope	Hans Lippershey	Netherlands	1608
Television:			
Iconoscope	Vladimir Zworykin	United States	1923
Televisor	John L. Baird	England	1925
Image dissector	Philo T. Farnsworth	United States	1928
Thermometer	Galileo Galilei	Italy	1593
Typewriter	Christopher Sholes	United States	1868
Vacuum tube	Lee De Forest	United States	1907
X-ray machine	Wilhelm K. Roentgen	Germany	1895
Zipper	Whitcomb L. Judson	United States	1893

INVERTEBRATES

There are hundreds of kinds of invertebrates.

INVERTEBRATES There are about a million kinds of animals. Only about 50,000 of them have backbones. The others are invertebrates—animals without backbones. Nineteen out of every 20 kinds of animals are invertebrates.

Invertebrates are all alike in not having backbones, but they are different from one another in other ways. They differ in the kinds of places in which they live, as well as the foods they eat, the ways they move, and the ways their bodies are built. And they differ greatly in size.

The simplest of the animals without backbones are the protozoa. Most of them are too small to be seen without a microscope. These tiny animals have only one cell in their whole body. Some kinds of protozoa live together in colonies. Others live by themselves. They breathe, digest food, and produce more like themselves, as all bigger animals do.

Sponges make up another group of invertebrates. They grow on the bottom of the ocean and let water currents bring them their food. A sponge is made up of many cells. A live sponge can be broken into a number of parts and each part will be able to live and grow by itself.

Another group of invertebrates have sacklike bodies. They have only one opening in the whole body. The jellyfish, sea anemones, and corals are animals of this

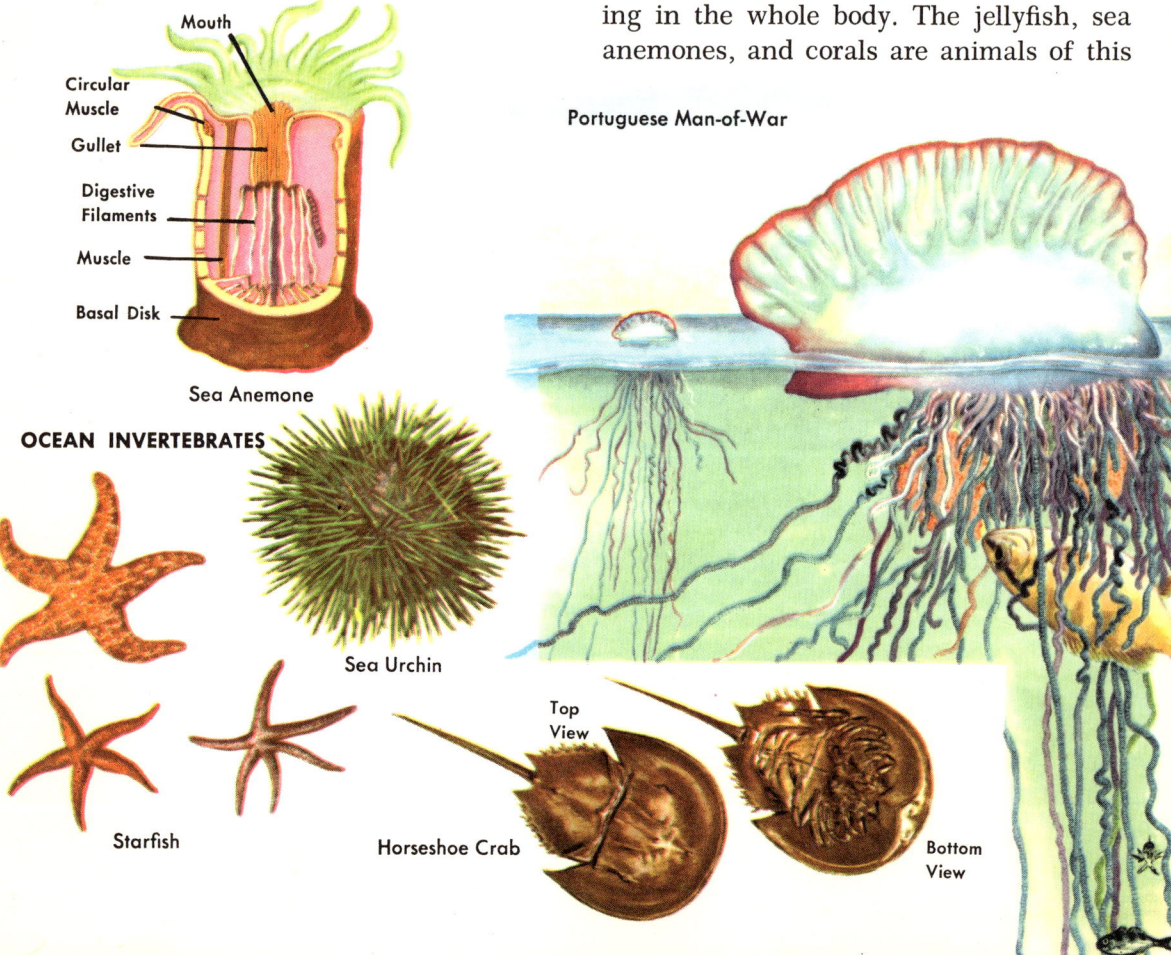

OCEAN INVERTEBRATES

kind. The Portuguese man-of-war belongs in this group. But it is not one animal. It is a whole colony of little animals. The gas-filled bag carries the whole colony along as it floats about.

Comb jellies are all sea animals. They get their name from "combs" made of tiny plates joined together like the teeth of a real comb. They move by moving their combs up and down.

There are thousands of kinds of worms. Some are flat; some are round and thread-like. Some have bodies divided into parts, or segments. Most people think of worms as ugly, and many of them are. But some sea worms look like gay flowers.

The animals of one very large group have shells. Snails, clams, squids, and all their close relatives are in this big group. Some have one-piece shells; others have two-piece shells.

Starfish belong to a group of spiny-skinned animals. Their bodies have spines all over them. The sea urchins, sand dollars, and sea cucumbers are close relatives of the starfish.

The jointed-legged animals make up by far the biggest group of invertebrates. All the insects belong in this group. More than half of all the kinds of animals there are, are insects. Here, too, are the shrimps, crabs, lobsters, barnacles, spiders, centipedes, and thousand-legs.

Many invertebrates are most unpopular. Some of the worms cause diseases in other animals. So do some protozoa. Insects may carry diseases, eat our foods, and harm our belongings. On the other hand, many animals without backbones are helpful to us. Silkworms furnish us silk, honeybees make honey, and crabs, lobsters, oysters, and shrimp are good seafoods. Others are helpful in other ways. Many thousands of kinds are neither helpful nor harmful. (See ANIMAL KINGDOM; CENTIPEDE; CRUSTACEANS; INSECTS; JELLYFISH; MOLLUSKS; PROTOZOA; SHELLFISH; SPONGES; STARFISH; WORMS.)

Kelps, which are brown algae, are one of the sources of iodine.

Kelps

IODINE The brown iodine we buy in drugstores is not pure iodine. It is iodine dissolved in alcohol. Pure iodine is a solid. It forms small, dark crystals. These crystals turn to a beautiful purple vapor when they are heated.

Our bodies have to have iodine. Goiter is a disease that is sometimes caused by not getting all we need. People who live near the seacoast seldom have goiter. They get enough iodine from fish and other sea food. People who live far from the sea often use iodized salt to make sure that they get enough iodine. Iodized salt is salt to which iodine has been added.

Much iodine is used in medicine. Chemists use a great deal, too.

Iodine is one of the simple substances called elements. It is never found pure in nature. It can be obtained from seaweed or from minerals found in the ground.

The people of ancient times did not know iodine. A French scientist first discovered it in 1811. He was trying to make gunpowder for Napoleon. He thought that he might be able to get one of the necessary materials from seaweed. In the seaweed he found iodine. (See ELEMENTS.)

IOWA

IOWA The name Iowa probably came from Indian words meaning "This is the place." Iowans of today can say proudly, "This is the state whose farmlands are worth more than those of any other state." They can say, too, that 99 out of every 100 adults in the state can read and write. No other state has so good a record.

As the small map shows, Iowa lies in the north-central section of the United States. It is between the Mississippi and Missouri rivers. In size, Iowa is almost exactly in the middle of the 50 states. Twenty-four states are larger, and 25 are smaller.

The Iowa country was visited in 1673 by the French explorers Joliet and Marquette. For many years it belonged either to Spain or to France. In 1803 Thomas Jefferson bought it from France as a part of the Louisiana Purchase. Pioneers began the settlement of Iowa in the 1830's. They came from the East and the South, some by river boat and some by covered wagon. The covered wagons were carried on ferryboats across the broad Mississippi to the Iowa shore. The settlers found their new homeland covered with tall prairie grass. There were few woods except near the rivers. The soil was very rich, and the land was nearly level. Before long newcomers arrived from many countries in Europe.

Iowa became a state in 1846. It was the 29th state to join the Union.

Today farmlands cover more than nine-tenths of Iowa. The countryside is dotted with well-kept, neatly painted farmhouses, barns, and silos. With modern farm machinery a farmer can easily cultivate ten times as much land as a pioneer farmer did with his horse-drawn plow.

Iowa farms furnish one-tenth of the whole nation's food. Iowa is a part of the great Corn Belt that runs from central Ohio westward to eastern Nebraska. The state is often called "the land where the tall corn grows." Nearly every year Iowa tops all other states in corn production. Iowa farmers feed much of the corn they raise to hogs. About one-fourth of all the hogs sold in the United States come from Iowa farms. Iowa farmers raise many beef cattle, too. The state leads the country in raising chickens and popcorn.

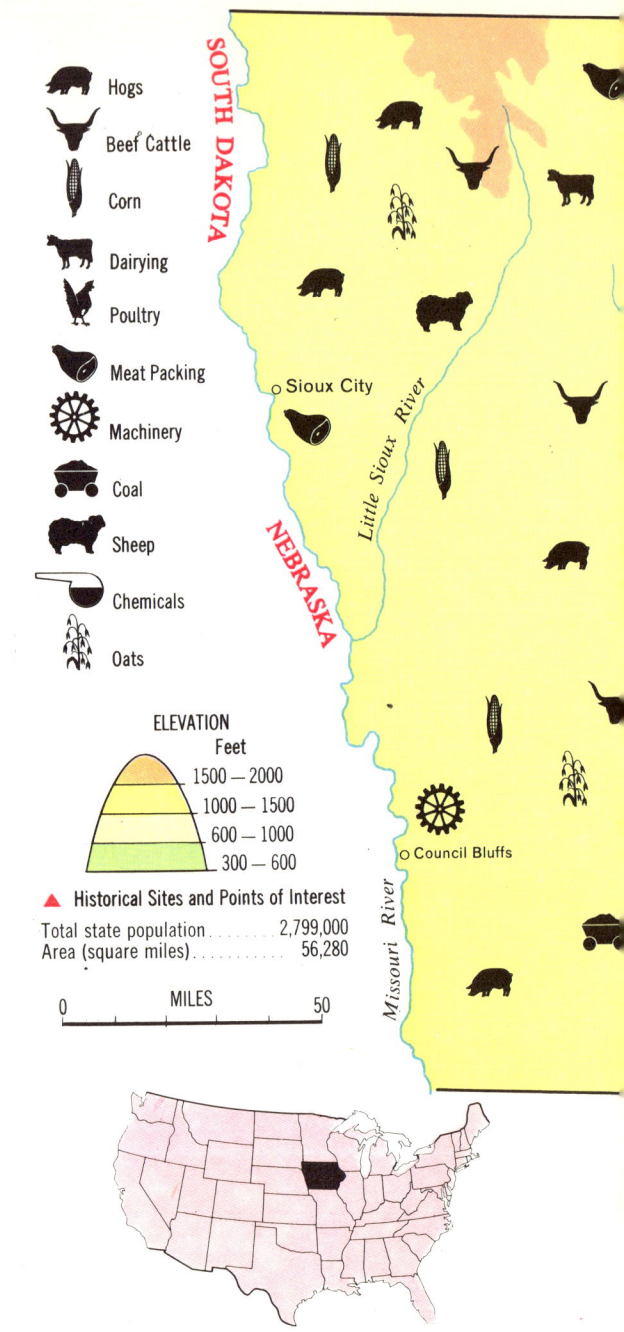

In Iowa's cities there are many factories. Iowa's farms and factories depend on each other. The factories make tractors and machinery for use on farms. From grain raised on the farms factories make many break-

IOWA

fast cereals. The Quaker Oats mill in Cedar Rapids is the largest cereal mill in the world. The most important Iowa industry, however, is meat-packing.

Iowa's chief cities are Des Moines, the capital, Sioux City, Davenport, Cedar Rapids, Dubuque, and Waterloo. Des Moines is the only city with a population of more than 100,000 people.

Iowa is called the "Hawkeye State." This name probably comes from the name of an Indian chief. But it may have come from the name of a scout in James Fenimore Cooper's *Leatherstocking Tales*.

IRAN

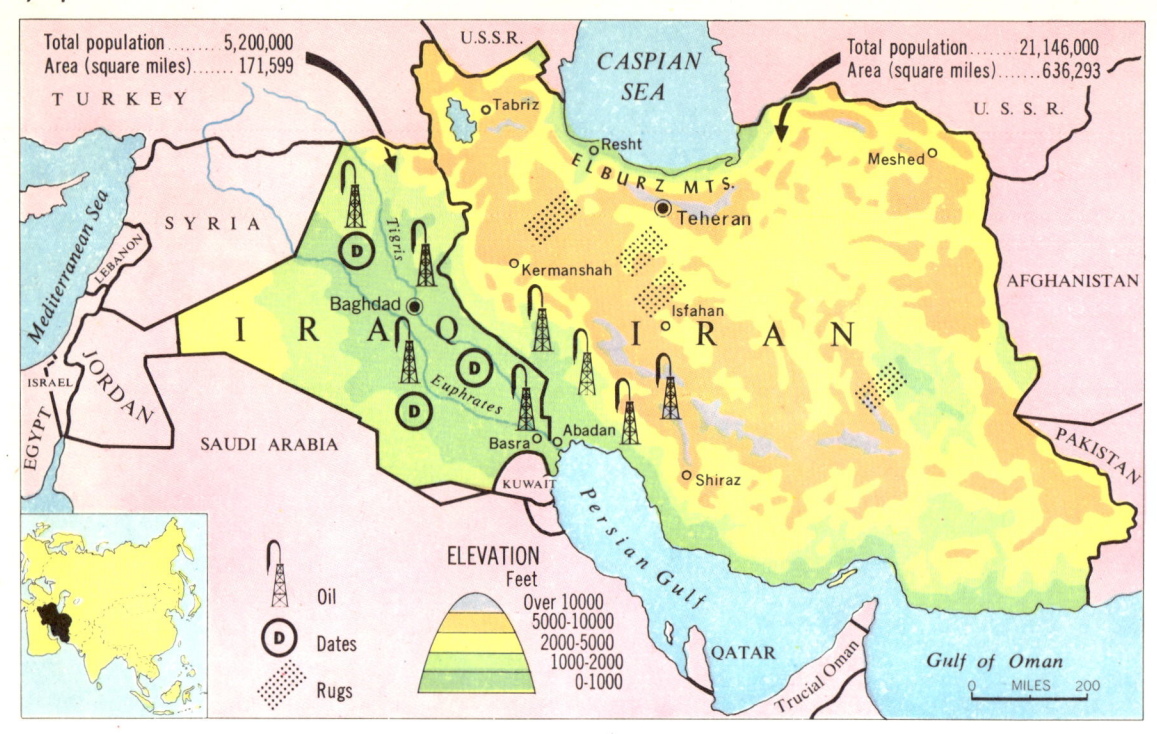

IRAN The part of Asia just east of the Mediterranean Sea is divided up into several countries. These countries make a bridge between Europe and central Asia, and between central Asia and Africa. In early days silk and spices from the Far East passed through them. Travel across them used to be by camel caravan. Now there are roads that trucks can travel. Airplanes, too, fly over them and stop at their airports. Oil is pumped over them through huge pipelines. Iran is one of the bridge countries. It used to be called Persia.

Iran is a dry land of many mountains. It is about one-sixth as big as the United States. Most of the people outside the cities are farmers or herders. Almost all the farmland has to be irrigated. The herders are mostly nomads who move about with their herds to find pasture.

Teheran, Iran's capital, is a big city. The old part has narrow streets and 12 gates. A fine new part has been added to the city. Iran's chief railroad runs through Teheran. It goes from the head of the Persian Gulf to the Caspian Sea.

Iran has great amounts of one thing to sell to other countries. It is oil. Carpets and hides are two of Iran's other exports. Among the things her people buy from abroad are cloth, sugar, and machinery.

Though it has a long history, Iran is young as a modern country. It is becoming more and more important because of its oil and its position in the Near East. (See HISTORY; NEAR EAST; PERSIA; PETROLEUM; SPICES.)

IRAQ The next-door neighbor of Iran is the smaller nation of Iraq. Iraq, too, is one of the bridge lands between the continents of Europe, Asia, and Africa.

This small country is the land once called Mesopotamia. Mesopotamia means "the land between the rivers." The two rivers are the Tigris and the Euphrates.

Here in the land between the rivers one of the world's oldest civilizations grew up. Scattered about there are still ruins of many cities of ancient times.

Iraq's capital is the famous old city of Baghdad. Many of the stories of the *Arabian Nights* are about Baghdad. It is a city of palm trees and bazaars and flat-roofed houses made of sun-dried brick. Many boats sail up and down the Tigris past Baghdad. Roads and caravan trails lead out in all directions from it. A railroad from Europe reaches it.

About four-fifths of all the world's supply of dates comes from Iraq. Along the two great rivers there are millions of date palms. The date orchards have to be irrigated. So does most of the farmland. Away from the rivers and cities the people of Iraq are herders.

Like Iran, Iraq has great oil fields. Big pipelines carry oil to the Mediterranean Sea to be loaded in tankers. Iraq, like Iran, is fast becoming an important modern country. In 1958, the people of Iraq overthrew their king. The country became a republic. (See BABYLONIA; DATES; NEAR EAST.)

IRELAND

NORTHERN IRELAND
Total population........1,397,000
Area (square miles)........5,459

Textiles
Potatoes
Fish
Dairying
Sheep
Beef Cattle

IRELAND
Total population........2,894,822
Area (square miles)........26,601

ELEVATION Feet
2000 – 5000
1000 – 2000
0 – 1000

IRELAND The island of Ireland is often called the Emerald Isle. The bright green of its many pastures is much like the green of emeralds. Ancestors of millions of Americans lived on the island. Each year many Americans visit it to see its beauty and the places told about in lovely Irish poems, songs, and stories.

For centuries, the country of Ireland spread over the whole island. Now a large part of the island is in the Republic of Ireland. Its capital is famous Dublin. The rest of the island is Northern Ireland. Belfast is its capital.

In what is now Northern Ireland, Scotch Protestants settled long ago. Most people there today are Protestants. Many are Scotch-Irish. In factories in and near Belfast very fine linens are made from flax grown near by. Irish linens travel to many lands. Belfast companies have built many giant ocean vessels.

Atlantic winds that drift across Ireland bring much gentle rain and winter warmth. They help to keep summers cool, too. In the big central lowland, there are thousands of farms. Potatoes and oats grow well. The island is poor in coal. But from bogs here and there men cut tons and tons of peat for fuel each year.

Nearly all the people in the Republic are Catholics. Most of them are farmers. Millions of cattle browse in their lowland pastures. In hillside pastures sheep graze. And Irish horses are famous. Milk helps to fatten for market millions of pigs to be seen near the little whitewashed stone cottages of the farmers. Much poultry is raised, too. Cattle, meat, butter, bacon, and eggs are chief exports. Most exports go to England. Lace made in Irish homes also goes abroad.

For centuries English landlords kept most of Ireland's farmers poor. Ireland was often called a land of potatoes, pigs, and poultry. Whenever the potato crop failed, famine drove Irish people to other lands. But after farmers could own their farms, they began to prosper.

The Irish are proud of new plans for improvements that will mean more good farmland. In Dublin and other places are many signs of great Irish achievements. (See BLARNEY STONE; BRITISH ISLES; LINEN; PEAT.)

Small white cottages dot Ireland.

IRON AND STEEL

IRON AND STEEL The Egyptians of 5,000 years ago made beads by shaping and polishing small pieces of a reddish rock containing iron. They thought of this rock as a precious stone just as they thought of turquoise. They had not learned to get the metal iron from this rock or any of the other rocks, or ores, in which it is found.

The common metal of the time was copper. From copper the Egyptians made tools and weapons, vases and bowls. Bronze, a mixture of copper and tin, in time took the place of copper. Later iron pushed bronze aside. Egypt fell from its greatness partly because it had no iron mines.

Steel, which is made from iron, is old, too, but not nearly as old as iron. In the days of the Crusades, Damascus was famous for its steel. Swords of Damascus steel helped win many a battle.

Today the people of the world use many, many millions of tons of iron and steel every year. We use iron and steel in so many ways that our lives would be very different if we had to give these metals up. In size, things made of iron and steel range all the way from tiny ball bearings only a fraction of an inch across to the heavy, strong framework of giant bridges, ships, and skyscrapers.

Perhaps the first iron that people used came from meteorites. At least some meteorites are made mostly from iron. Of course, there are not many meteorites. If all iron had to come from meteorites, it would be a precious metal. Most of the core of the earth is believed to be iron, but this iron is too deep for us to get. The iron of today comes from iron ore.

A rock is called an iron ore if it has a great deal of iron in it and can be made to give up its iron rather easily. In iron ore the iron is joined with at least one other material. It is, as scientists say, in a chemical compound.

One common iron ore is called hematite. This is the ore the Egyptians used for beads. Two other ores are magnetite and limonite. In all three of these ores the iron is joined with oxygen. Getting the iron from them means getting rid of the oxygen.

No one knows who first learned to get iron from iron ore. Perhaps thousands of years ago a man put some reddish rocks around his outdoor fire to protect it from the winds. And perhaps the flames, fanned by the wind, made the rocks so hot that the iron in them melted and ran down in a little stream. When it cooled it was a solid chunk of iron. This story may be far from the truth, but we do know that by 1500 B.C. an ancient people living in the Near East were heating iron ore and getting iron from it. They used bellows to blow air into the fire so that it would be very hot.

Today iron is taken from its ores in great blast furnaces. A blast furnace is a tall tower, often as tall as a ten-story building. It is made of steel and lined inside with firebrick. The "door" of the furnace is at the top. Reaching up to it are sloping tracks. Little cars run up and down these tracks every few minutes to feed iron ore, coke, and limestone into the furnace. An important part is played by the coke and limestone in getting the iron from the ore.

Every child has toys made of steel.

IRON AND STEEL

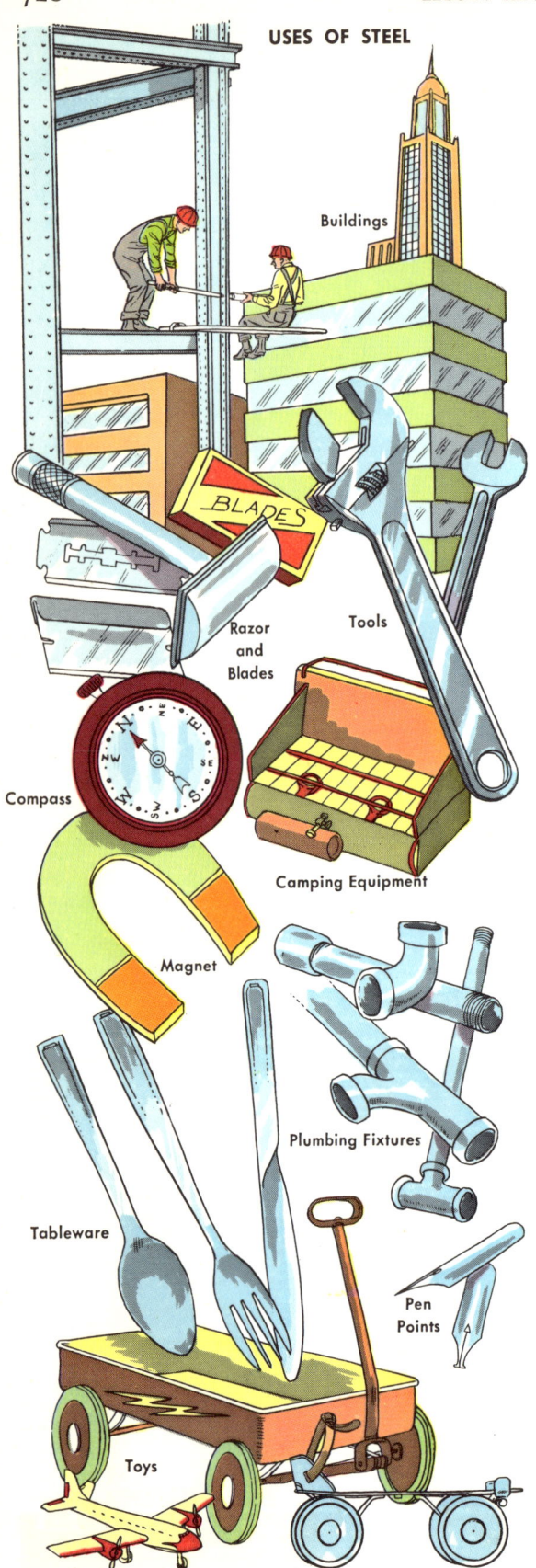

USES OF STEEL

Buildings · Tools · Razor and Blades · Compass · Camping Equipment · Magnet · Plumbing Fixtures · Tableware · Pen Points · Toys

Alongside every blast furnace there are three or four other towerlike structures. These are stoves. In them air is heated to about 1,200° F. Powerful blowing machines force a blast of this hot air into the furnace through pipes near the bottom. It is easy to see why the furnace is called a blast furnace.

The hot air heats the materials inside the blast furnace and causes chemical changes that raise the temperature inside the furnace to over 3,000° F. This is higher than the melting point of iron.

In one of the changes the coke, which is almost pure carbon, takes oxygen out of the iron ore. The oxygen joins the carbon to form carbon dioxide. Carbon dioxide is a gas; it escapes through the pipes near the top of the furnace. The melted iron drips down and collects in a pool at the bottom of the furnace.

In another change, the limestone takes away impurities in the ore and the coke. This change causes another liquid called slag to form. The slag is lighter than the melted iron and collects on top of it.

Every few hours the blast furnace is tapped. Tapping means taking out the iron and the slag. The iron comes out of one opening, the slag out of another. They flow into containers called ladles that stand on tracks beside the furnace. A blast furnace goes on working day and night until it has to be shut down for repairs.

Some of the liquid, red-hot iron is poured into molds. It hardens into chunks called pigs. They got this name because their shape reminded ironmakers of little pigs. Pigs of iron can be shipped anywhere to anyone who wants iron.

Some of the liquid iron goes at once to be made into steel. Making steel means taking out more impurities and adding at least carbon and usually other substances to it. Since steel is a mixture of a metal with other substances, it is an alloy.

There are many, many kinds of steel, and each kind has its special recipe. To

IRON AND STEEL

make stainless steel, for instance, rather large amounts of chromium and nickel are added to the iron and carbon mixture. Other metals may be added, too. Tungsten makes steel harder. Molybdenum (mo LIB de num) added to steel keeps certain chemicals from harming it.

Iron is made into steel in different kinds of furnaces. Much of it is now made in open-hearth furnaces. For a time most of the steel in the United States was made in Bessemer converters, but now less than a tenth is made in these converters. The finest steels are made in electric furnaces.

Steelmaking calls for great watchfulness. One reason the Bessemer converter was given up was that the steel was made so fast that there was no time to test it carefully during the making. Open-hearth furnaces and electric furnaces are slower. All the materials to be added are weighed carefully. If a cook were as careful about making a cake she could not measure the baking powder and flour and sugar in spoonfuls or cupfuls. She would have to get the amount right to within a ten-thousandth of an ounce.

When the steel leaves the furnaces it is poured into molds to harden into blocks called ingots. The ingots then go to soaking pits. There they are heated to just the right temperature to be shaped in rolling mills into any shape wanted by the users of steel. The steel from the rolling mills of the United States finds its way each year into thousands of railway cars, millions of automobiles, billions of "tin" cans, and countless other things.

In steel mills machines now do much of the dangerous work that once was done by people. There are safeguards to protect the workers. Perhaps most important of all, the workers are taught what the dangers are and how to guard against them. (See ALLOYS; BRIDGES; BUILDING MATERIALS; COMPOUNDS; ELEMENTS; METALS; MINES AND MINING; SAFETY; SKYSCRAPERS.)

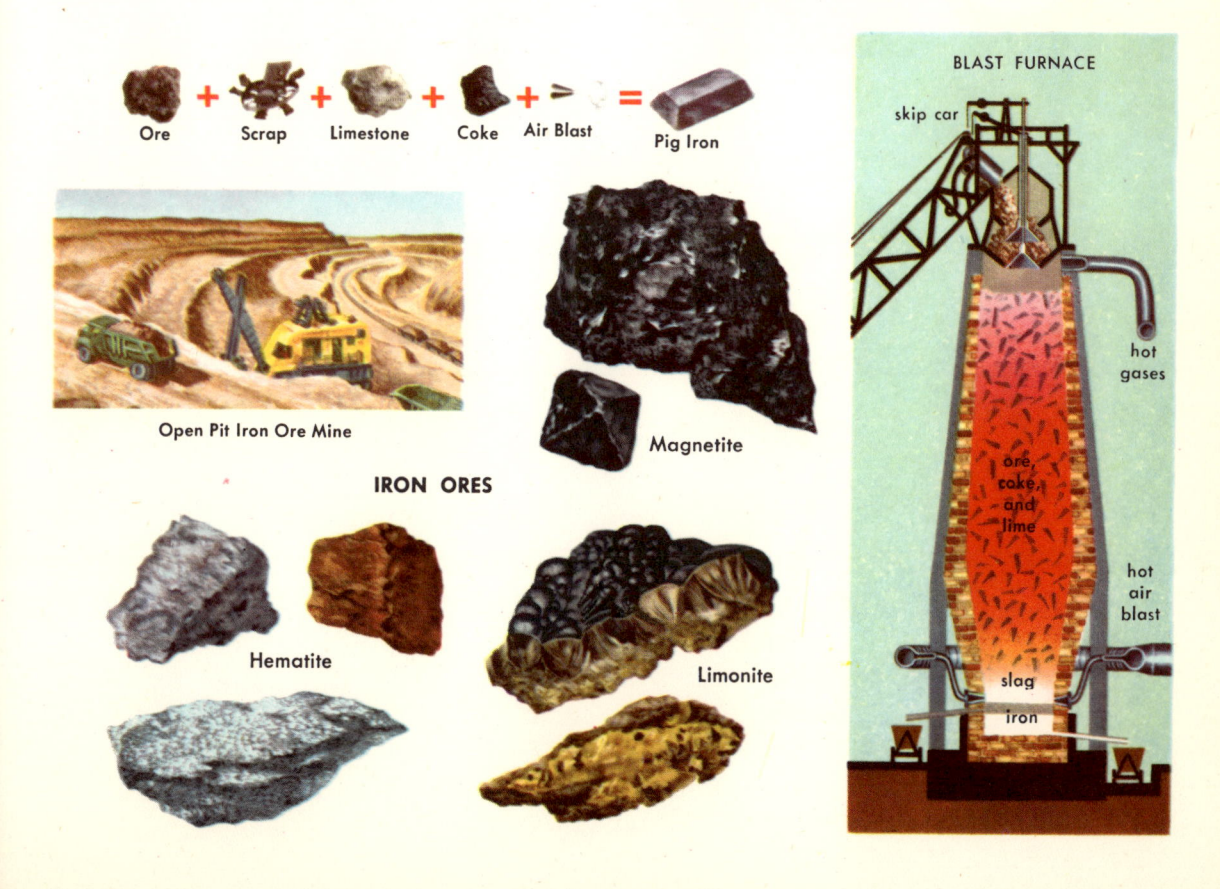

Ore + Scrap + Limestone + Coke + Air Blast = Pig Iron

Open Pit Iron Ore Mine

IRON ORES

Magnetite

Hematite

Limonite

BLAST FURNACE

skip car

hot gases

ore, coke, and lime

hot air blast

slag

iron

Portable Iron Lung

Tank-type Iron Lung

IRON LUNG To stay alive a person has to breathe. He must take air into his lungs and breathe it out again. Muscles are used in breathing. They squeeze air out of the lungs. Then they make the lungs expand so that fresh air is drawn in.

When a person has polio, the muscles that help him breathe may not work as they should. The iron lung was invented to help such people. Hospitals that treat polio patients have iron lungs.

The iron lung is a big iron case which encloses the patient's chest. An electric motor makes air move into and out of the case. The changing pressure on the outside of the patient's chest does the work of his muscles and makes him breathe.

A patient who lives in an iron lung for a while may get well and not need it any longer. But some people who have had polio have spent years in an iron lung.

The iron lung was invented in 1928. It has saved the lives of thousands of people. (See BREATHING; POLIOMYELITIS.)

IRRIGATION Some of our farms and gardens are in places that were once desert. In most deserts there is enough rain for some plants but not enough for the plants we raise. People have turned desert land into farms and gardens by bringing water to it. Much desert land can be made to raise crops if it can get enough water. Watering dry land so that it will grow crops is called irrigation.

Long ago the ancient Egyptians and Babylonians irrigated their fields by dipping water out of wells or out of the great rivers that flowed through their lands. Sometimes they used oxen or camels to help them raise and lower the pails or skin bags they used as dippers. The water flowed to the plants in the fields through small ditches that had been dug. In some parts of the world land is still irrigated in this simple way.

Rice fields must be flooded part of the time.

IRRIGATION

In other places there are great irrigation systems. Dams built across rivers form huge reservoirs for irrigation water. This water goes out from the reservoirs to the places where it is needed. It may travel in open canals and ditches or through underground tunnels or pipes.

In the United States many millions of acres of land are irrigated. Dozens of big dams and reservoirs have been built. The largest reservoir is Lake Mead on the border between Arizona and Nevada. The second-tallest dam in the world—Hoover Dam—was built across the Colorado River to form this reservoir. Hoover Dam was formerly called Boulder Dam. Other great dams in America are the Grand Coulee, the Hungry Horse, and the Fort Peck.

Water stored for irrigation helps in another way, too. As it flows from the reservoirs it drives great water wheels that turn electric generators. Almost every big dam has a big power plant beside it. (See DAMS; WATER SUPPLY.)

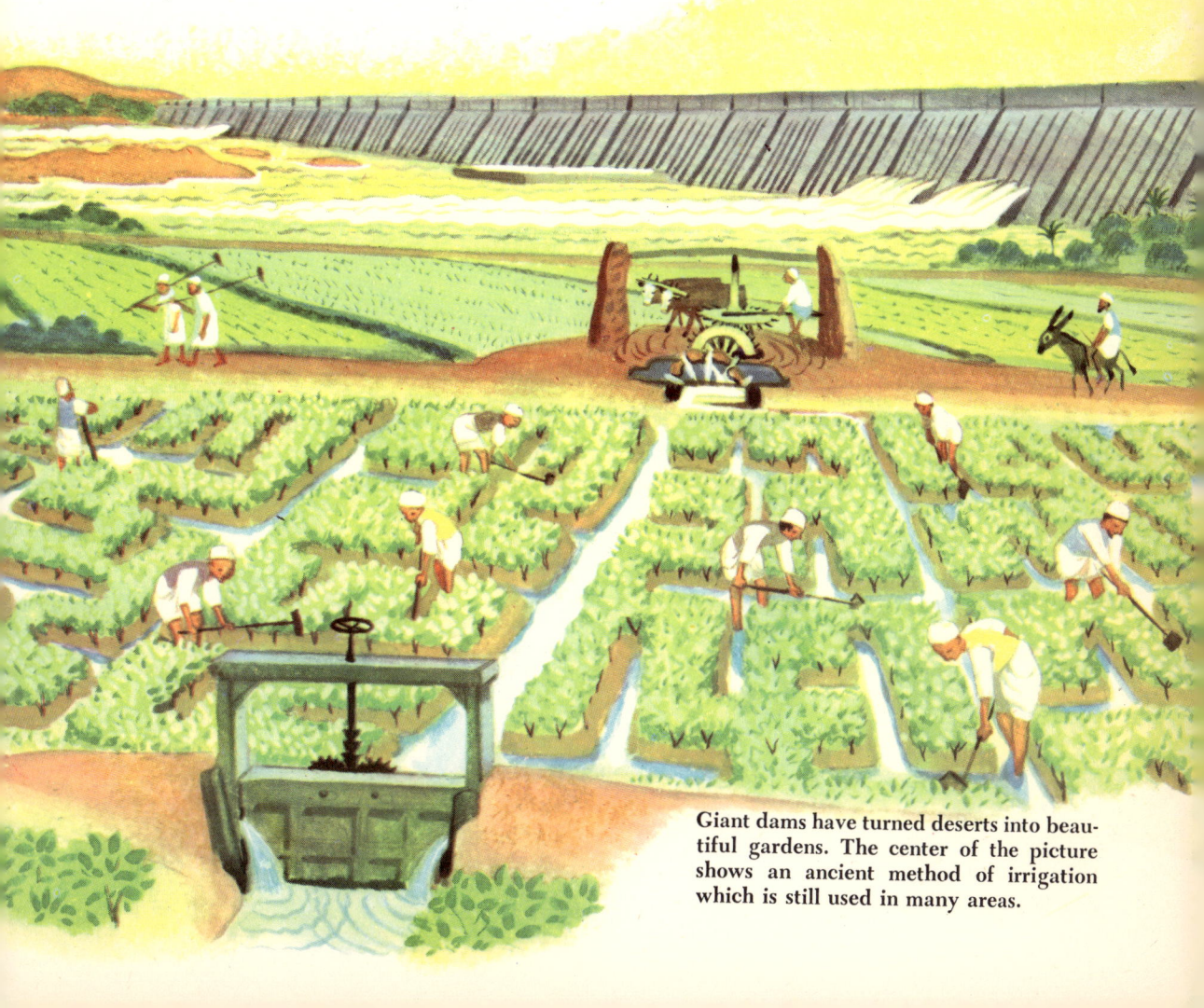

Water from deep wells is sometimes used for irrigation.

Giant dams have turned deserts into beautiful gardens. The center of the picture shows an ancient method of irrigation which is still used in many areas.

Life of Columbus

"The Bold Dragoon"
Tales of a Traveler

"The Christmas Dinner"
The Sketch Book

"Rip Van Winkle"
The Sketch Book

IRVING, WASHINGTON (1783-1859) Almost every American boy or girl knows the stories of Rip Van Winkle's long sleep and Ichabod Crane's attempt to escape from the headless horseman. Washington Irving wrote these stories about 150 years ago. Irving is often called the father of American literature. He was the first American writer to be honored in Europe.

As a boy Irving lived in the city of New York. He was not a strong child. One of the things he liked to do best was to listen to stories told by the descendants of the early Dutch settlers of New York. When later he began writing, he did not use his own name. He used a Dutch name instead—Diedrich Knickerbocker.

After he grew up, Irving spent much of his time abroad. Some of his writing is about people and places in Europe. But his most famous books are those about America. They tell many of the stories he heard as a boy. His best stories are in *The Sketch Book*. (See ALHAMBRA; AMERICAN WRITERS; LITERATURE.)

ISLAM The religion with the second-largest number of followers in the world is Islam. This religion is sometimes known as Mohammedanism because its founder was Mohammed. But Moslems—as believers in Islam are called—do not worship Mohammed. They simply believe he was a prophet of God.

Followers of Islam are scattered throughout the world. It is the leading religion in countries in North Africa, the Middle East, and in the East Indies.

There are ways in which Islam is like the Christian and Jewish religions. Moslems believe in the same God the Christians and Jews believe in, but their name for him is Allah. The Koran, which is the sacred book of the Moslems, is based partly on the Old and New Testaments and partly on the teachings of Mohammed. Jesus and many of the prophets of the Bible are mentioned frequently in the Koran. Most of the Ten Commandments of the Bible also have a place in the Koran. Moslems believe that the main difference between their religion and that of the Christians and Jews is in their ideas of the true meanings of the Old and New Testaments.

Moslems worship in churches called mosques. Many of these mosques are among the world's most beautiful buildings. (See MOHAMMED; RELIGIONS OF THE WORLD.)

ISLAND

ISLAND An island is land with water all around it. There are many thousands of islands in seas and lakes and rivers.

"When is an island not an island?" would make a good riddle. The answer would be, "When it is a continent." Australia has water all around it, but it is so big that it is called a continent.

The number of islands changes. Some small islands are the tops of volcanoes that rise up from the bottom of the sea. A volcano under the sea may erupt and make itself so tall that it reaches up above the water. Then there is a new island. A volcano may erupt and blow off its head. Then an island may disappear.

Not all islands are the tops of volcanoes. Some are the tops of other mountains. Some are built up by small animals called corals. Some are the higher regions of areas that have sunk below the sea. Many river islands are built of sand and mud that have been dropped by the river.

The chart lists the world's biggest islands.

ISLAND	OCEAN	AREA (Sq. Mi.)	POPULATION
Greenland	N. Atlantic / Arctic	840,000	24,000
New Guinea	Pacific	340,000	2,490,000
Borneo	Pacific	290,000	2,900,000
Madagascar	Indian	228,000	4,500,000
Baffin	Arctic	198,000	3,000
Sumatra	Indian	164,000	11,100,000
Great Britain	Atlantic	89,000	49,500,000
Honshu	Pacific	88,000	67,300,000
Victoria	Arctic	80,000	
Ellesmere	Arctic	77,000	60
Celebes	Pacific	73,000	5,600,000
South Island (New Zealand)	Pacific	58,000	677,000
Java	Pacific	49,000	55,000,000
Cuba	Atlantic	44,000	6,000,000
North Island (New Zealand)	Pacific	44,000	1,500,000

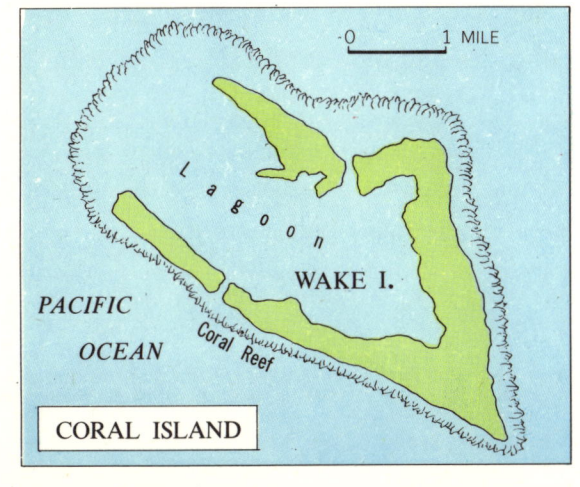

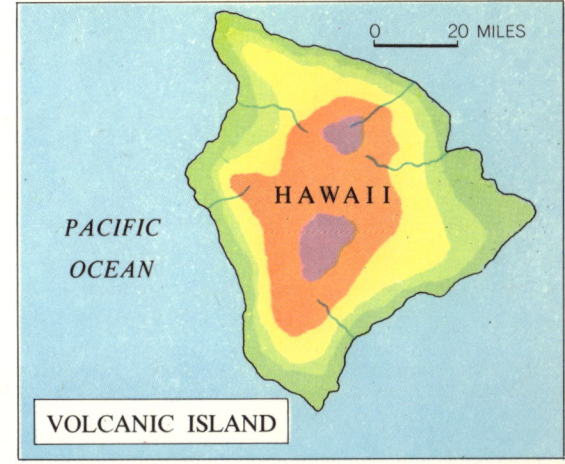

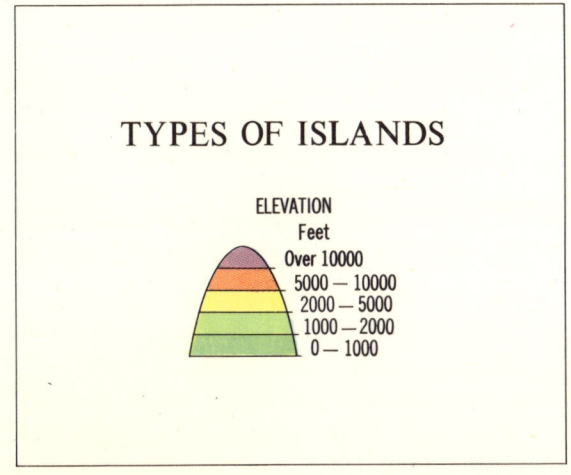

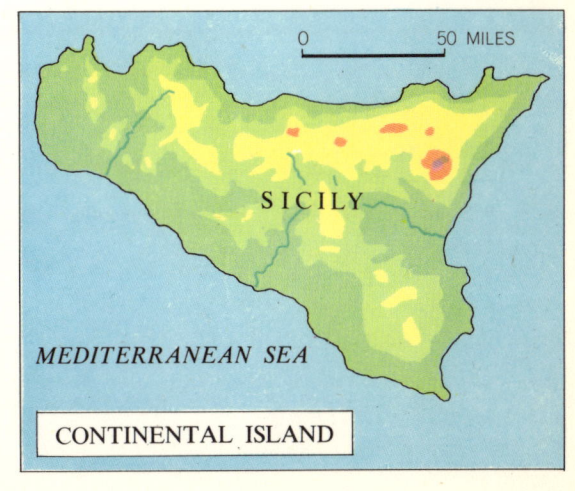

CORAL ISLAND

VOLCANIC ISLAND

TYPES OF ISLANDS

ELEVATION Feet
Over 10000
5000 – 10000
2000 – 5000
1000 – 2000
0 – 1000

CONTINENTAL ISLAND

ISRAEL

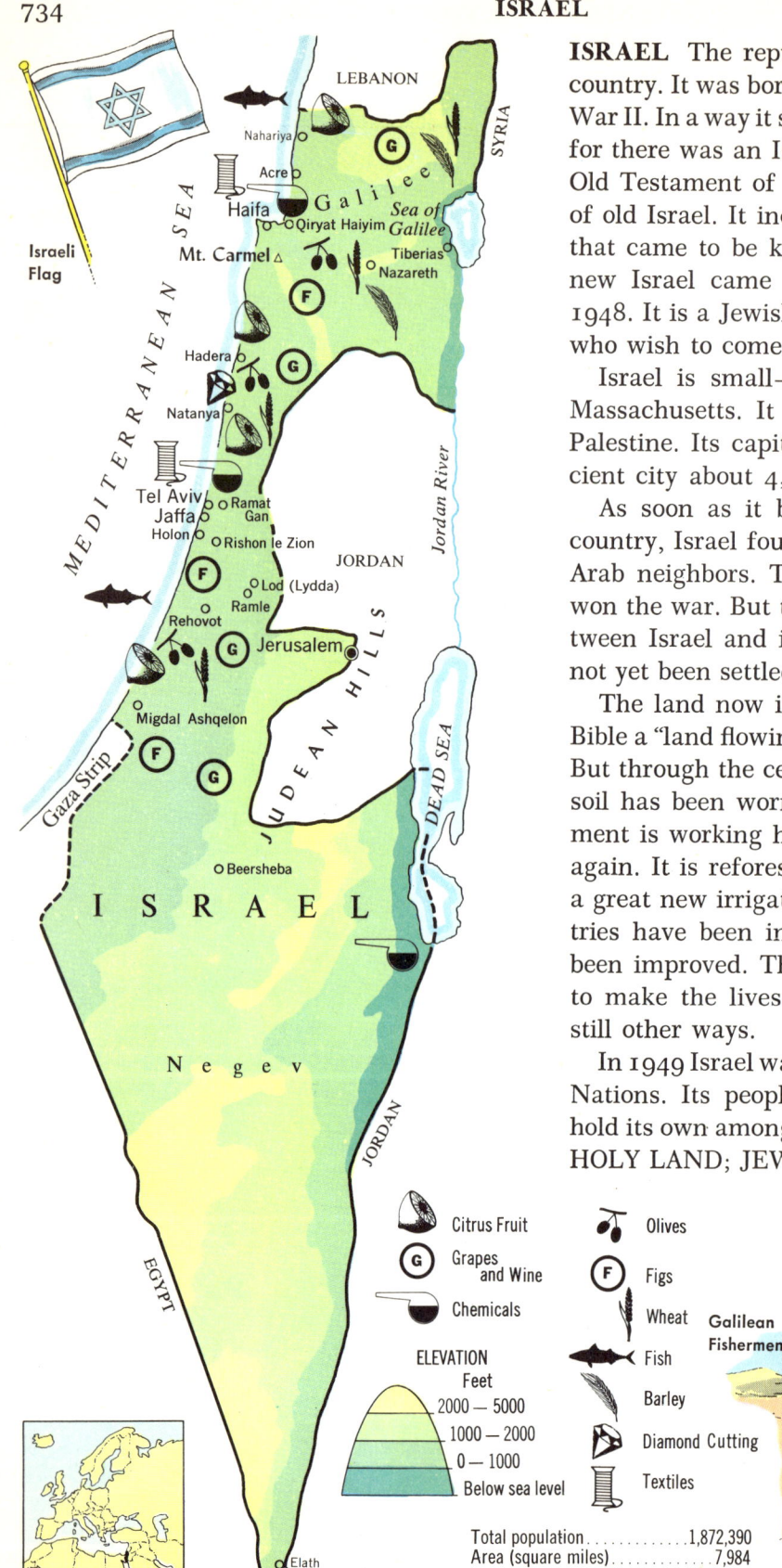

ISRAEL The republic of Israel is a new country. It was born after the end of World War II. In a way it should not be called new, for there was an Israel centuries ago. The Old Testament of the Bible tells the story of old Israel. It included most of the land that came to be known as Palestine. The new Israel came into existence in May, 1948. It is a Jewish state, open to all Jews who wish to come to it.

Israel is small—not quite as large as Massachusetts. It does not take in all of Palestine. Its capital is Jerusalem, an ancient city about 4,000 years old.

As soon as it became an independent country, Israel found itself at war with its Arab neighbors. The young country soon won the war. But the exact boundaries between Israel and its Arab neighbors have not yet been settled.

The land now in Israel is called in the Bible a "land flowing with milk and honey." But through the centuries much of Israel's soil has been worn out. The new government is working hard to build the soil up again. It is reforesting land and planning a great new irrigation system. New industries have been introduced. Schools have been improved. The government is trying to make the lives of its people better in still other ways.

In 1949 Israel was admitted to the United Nations. Its people feel sure that it can hold its own among the other nations. (See HOLY LAND; JEWS; NEAR EAST.)

Total population............1,872,390
Area (square miles)............7,984

Towers of Rumeli Hisari

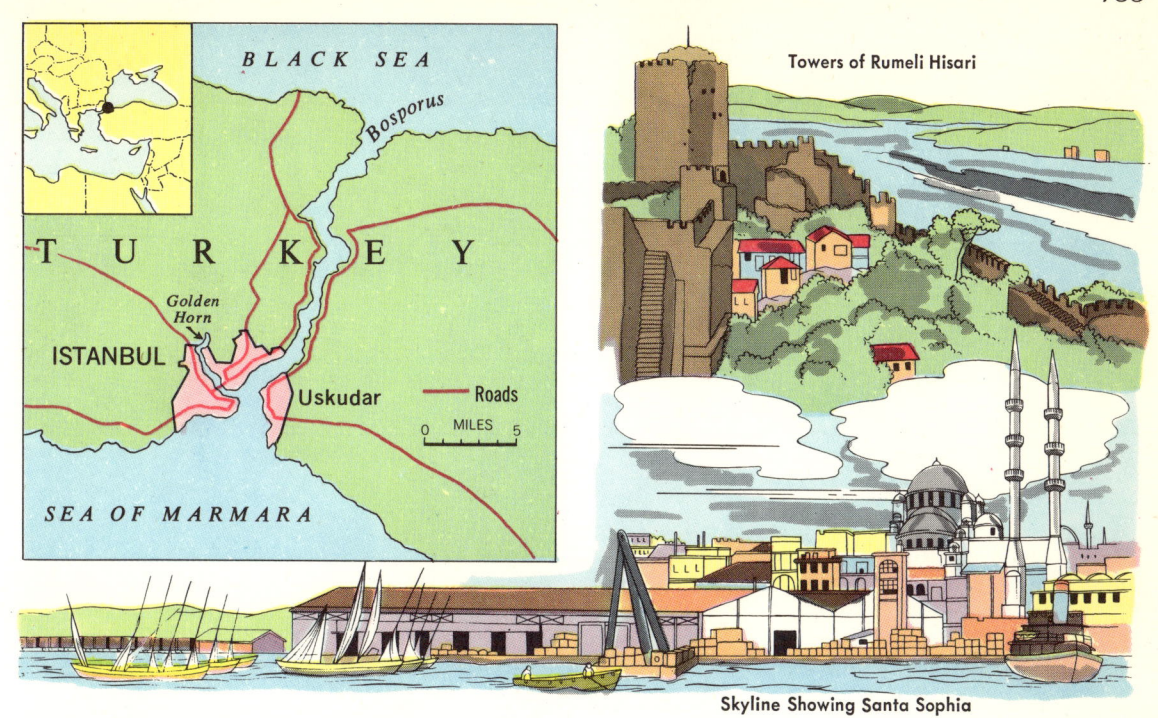

Skyline Showing Santa Sophia

ISTANBUL The city of Istanbul is the largest city of Turkey. Part of Istanbul is in Europe and part in Asia. The two parts are separated by the strait called the Bosporus. A long, narrow bay called the Golden Horn extends into the European part of Istanbul from the Sea of Marmara.

Istanbul was founded by the Greeks in about 660 B.C. They called it Byzantium.

The city was at a great crossroads. Travelers between Europe and Asia crossed the Bosporus there. Travelers between the Mediterranean and the Black Sea sailed by.

In A.D. 196 the Romans captured the city. Later the Roman emperor Constantine made it the capital of the Roman Empire. He named it Constantinople.

As Constantinople, the city had a stormy history and saw many wars. It was one of the battlefields of the Crusades.

The Turks won Constantinople in 1453. From then on for nearly 500 years it was the capital of Turkey. It was the capital, in a sense, of the whole Mohammedan world.

When Turkey became a republic in 1922 Ankara became its capital. The republic also officially changed the name of Constantinople to Istanbul.

Although Istanbul is no longer the capital of Turkey, it is still a great city, with more than a million people. It has many modern buildings. But signs of its long history remain. (See BOSPORUS; TURKEY.)

ISTHMUS An isthmus is a narrow neck of land joining two big bodies of land. It may join two continents. It may join a peninsula to the mainland of a continent.

Two famous isthmuses are the Isthmus of Suez and the Isthmus of Panama. The Isthmus of Suez joins Africa and Asia. The Isthmus of Panama joins North and South America. These isthmuses once greatly hindered ocean travel. Now canals have been dug across both of them. (See PANAMA CANAL; SUEZ CANAL.)

736 ITALY

ITALY

ITALY As the map shows, Italy fills a bootlike peninsula that reaches southward into the Mediterranean Sea. It also stretches northward to the Alps. A plane would have to fly 760 miles to fly from the northernmost place in it to the southernmost. Italy is one of the larger of the many countries of Europe. And of all those countries, only the Soviet Union, Britain, and Germany have more people. In each of three of Italy's cities, more than 1,000,000 people live. One of those three cities is Rome, the capital of Italy.

Rome, on the Tiber River, is a very old city. Some 2,000 years ago it was the capital of an empire that included what is now Italy and all the other land that borders the Mediterranean. Several centuries later that great empire was broken up.

The next great period for Italy was between 1300 and 1500. Its cities became leaders among the cities of Europe. From Venice and Genoa great fleets went out to trade with other lands. Italian craftsmen made beautiful cloth, glass, leatherwork, and jewelry. Merchants became very wealthy. Some founded banks much like those of today. They made loans even to kings and queens. Italian scholars rediscovered the learning of the ancient Greeks. Italian painters, sculptors, architects, and writers grew famous. Ideas about commerce, art, and learning spread from Italy to other countries of Europe. And still today along the narrow streets of Florence and the canals of Venice one can see palaces of merchants of those days. In the churches and museums one sees marvelous and beautiful works of art.

During this time Italy was made up of many small city-states. Not until 1870 were they united into one country. After World War II Italy became a republic. It includes Sicily and Sardinia. Rome now is both its capital and a center of railroads, highways, and airlines. Ancient buildings and ruins there stand side by side with modern hotels and apartment buildings. A new steel-and-glass railroad station stands where baths of a Roman emperor stood. Automobiles and streetcars roll through the gateways of the third-century city walls. Near the coast northwest of Rome, beautiful white marble still is cut from ancient quarries.

Southeast of Rome is Naples, the chief port for Rome and the peninsula. Its new and old parts overlook a fine harbor, the blue Bay of Naples. On the outskirts are modern mills. Not far away are famous Vesuvius and Amalfi Drive.

For northern Italy, Genoa rather than Venice is now the chief port. Italian goods move more to western Europe and the Americas than to the Orient. Italy, it is said, has turned its back on the Adriatic Sea to the east. But Venice attracts many tourists. Genoa manufactures aluminum and ships. Guides show visitors the house where Columbus was born.

Milan is the chief rail and industrial center of the north. Turin is Italy's "Detroit." These cities and many others on the northern plain use electricity generated in great water-driven power plants in the Alps. A large part of the Italian railway system is electrified. Italy lacks coal.

The northern plain is the most thickly settled part of Italy. The farmers there have level land, rich soil, and summer rains. The floor of the great Po Valley is covered with fields of corn, wheat, rice, and sugar beets. Farmers in the mountainous peninsula have dry, hot summers and winter rains. They grow "Mediterranean" crops—macaroni wheat, olives, grapes, oranges, and lemons. Italian farm families are thrifty and hard working. With little or no modern farm machinery they get big yields per acre. Italians love beauty. Even on steep slopes of the Apennine Mountains, fields, orchards, and pastures are well kept. (See CAESARS; DICTATORS; EXPLORERS; GALILEO; HISTORY; LEANING TOWER OF PISA; PAINTERS AND PAINTING; POMPEII; RENAISSANCE; ROME, ANCIENT; SCULPTURE; VESUVIUS.)

The walrus' ivory tusk is useful to the Eskimo.

IVORY Most of the hard, creamy-white substance called ivory comes from the tusks of African elephants. The ivory in the tusks of a big elephant may weigh as much as 200 pounds. Some ivory is found buried in the ground in northern countries. It comes from the tusks of mammoths and mastodons that lived there thousands of years ago during the great Ice Age. A little ivory comes from walrus tusks.

Ivory can be carved easily. It can be beautifully polished, too. It is used for billiard balls, piano keys, chessmen, knife handles, and many other such things.

People have used ivory ever since the days of the cave men. The Egyptians had many beautiful ivory objects, and India has long been famous for its intricate ivory carvings. King Solomon, the Bible tells us, had a whole throne carved out of ivory. (See PLASTICS.)

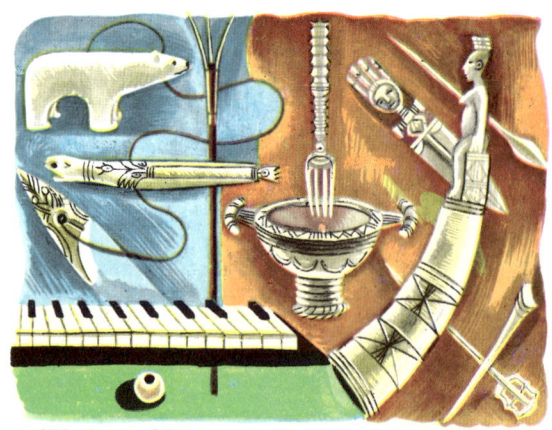

USES OF IVORY

J · JAPAN

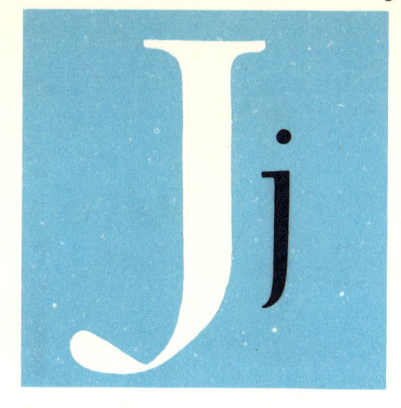

The letter *J* is only a few hundred years old. *J* now does not sound at all like *I*, but in the beginning it was just a decorated *I*. The Romans usually made their *I* just as we do today. But sometimes they added a curve at the bottom to make it look better. They might write the number 3, which they wrote with *I*'s, this way: IIJ. Not till the 17th century were *I* and *J* separate letters.

In almost all English words with a *J*, the *J* stands for the sound it has in *just*. This is exactly the same sound *G* stands for in *giant*. In *hallelujah j* has a *y* sound instead.

JADE Many beautiful ornaments are carved of jade. Jade is one of the gem minerals. But it is not as rare and expensive as diamonds and emeralds. It is one of the semiprecious stones.

Jade is found chiefly in the Far East. The Chinese were carving beautiful things of jade before the time of Christ. They carved many figures for their temples. The Chinese almost worshiped jade itself. To them this mineral stood for all the virtues.

Some jade is mined, but much of it is found in streams. Marco Polo watched Chinese workers hunt for jade when he made his famous trip to China. The men waded in streams and felt for pebbles and boulders of jade with their bare feet.

Time did not mean much to the early Chinese artists who made ornaments of jade. Jade is not easy to carve. A Chinese artist might spend his whole life carving a beautiful jade ornament.

The Aztecs of Mexico prized jade, too. Two of the gifts which their emperor Montezuma sent to Cortés to persuade him to go back to Spain were pieces of jade. They were worth, the Aztecs said, two whole cartloads of gold.

Today many thousands of dollars can be spent for a jade ornament. The carving, of course, is worth more than the jade itself. The pictures show that all jade is not the same color. The color seen most often is green. It is the color called jade green. (See AZTECS; GEMS.)

JAPAN The Japanese are island people. Their country lies in the North Pacific near the mainland of Asia. It is a long string of hundreds of islands, many of them tiny. Most of the Japanese people live on the four largest islands.

Japan has a long history. The first Japanese emperor began to rule about 660 B.C. During its long history armies came from the mainland many times to try to conquer Japan. They all failed, but Japan did allow ideas to come to her from the mainland. Her people learned, chiefly from the Chinese, much about writing, art, religion, and architecture. Japanese merchants traded with mainland merchants. The traders and pirates of Japan ruled the Far Eastern seas.

In the 16th century traders from Europe came to these waters. The Japanese were afraid of these strangers. To protect themselves they shut all foreigners out of Japan and locked themselves in for 200 years.

In 1853 Commodore Perry of the United States Navy, with four naval vessels, arrived in Japan. To the Emperor he brought gifts made in America, among them a telegraph set and a model of a locomotive. He persuaded the Emperor to "open up" Japan. Soon the Japanese were taking on western ways—building factories, railroads, and

JADE

Australian

Early Chinese (Carved)

Tibetan

schools; playing baseball and tennis; taking part in their own government by voting. With a strong army and navy the Japanese gradually enlarged their empire. But they lost their new lands in World War II.

Japan is a little smaller than California. Most of it is mountainous. Only a sixth of it can be used for farming. But it has about half as many people as big United States. Though the Japanese love their beautiful country, green with crops and forests, it is hard for so many people to make a living there. Japan is one of the world's most crowded countries.

The big island of Hokkaido is not very crowded. It has short summers and long, snowy winters much like those of the state of Maine. Hokkaido farms are large, as Japanese farms go. They measure about ten acres. The farmers raise hay and a kind of rice that ripens in the short summer. There are dairy farms and forests.

Climate in the other three big islands is much like the climate of the Carolinas and Georgia. Farms are only two or three acres in size. About half of all the farmland is used for growing rice in tiny irrigated fields. Rice is Japan's chief food crop. Besides growing rice in summer, farmers raise winter crops such as wheat in most of the rice fields. They have to work very hard. There are some hillside fields of tea. Except on dairy farms near cities, there are not many farm animals in Japan.

On these three islands most separate houses are made of wood. Parts of the inside and outside walls are sliding panels. On warm days the panels are opened. The floor is covered with reed mats. Japanese do not like to have much furniture. Most homes now have electric lights. Some have sewing machines and radios.

Japan is the greatest fishing country in the world. Waters around the islands are full of fish. Japanese families eat fish and rice almost every day.

Tokyo, Japan's capital, is the world's largest city. It has more than 8,000,000 people. Railroads and bus lines connect it with many other cities. In hundreds of city factories, and in homes, too, the industrious Japanese do much manufacturing. Silk from silkworms raised in farm homes is used in making silk cloth. Cloth, machines, chemicals, china, and paper are among important Japanese products. But the number of Japanese farmers is greater than the number of Japanese factory and trade workers together.

Trade with other nations of the world is very important to Japan now. It must sell in order to buy raw materials its factories need. Japan's best customer is the United States, and Japan is America's best customer in Asia. (See OSAKA; TOKYO; WORLD WAR II.)

Jefferson's home is called Monticello.

JEFFERSON, THOMAS (1743-1826) Four of the first five presidents of the United States came from the state of Virginia. Thomas Jefferson, the third president, was one of them. Monticello, his beautiful home, is still one of the most fascinating show places of Virginia.

Jefferson would be famous even if he had never been elected president. For he wrote the Declaration of Independence.

In the early days of planning the new country many Americans, although they did not want to be under the king of England, wanted their country to have a king. Jefferson worked hard against this idea. He believed that the people would be wise enough to choose good rulers.

When Jefferson became president, the United States went only as far west as the Mississippi River. During his term Jefferson bought from France nearly a million square miles of land west of the Mississippi. This land was called the Louisiana Purchase. Many states were made from it. Getting this land was one of the most important single acts of Jefferson as president.

Jefferson had a great many interests. He liked science and music. He was a good architect. He was also interested in schools. After his two terms as president, he founded the University of Virginia. Everyone agrees he was a really great American. (See DECLARATION OF INDEPENDENCE; PATRIOTS; PRESIDENTS.)

Speckled Jellyfish

JELLYFISH The body of a jellyfish looks as if it were made of jelly. It is easy to see, then, how jellyfish got the "jelly" in their name. It is not easy to see how they got the "fish" in their name, for they are not much like fish, except that they do live in water.

Most jellyfish have an umbrella-shaped body. Under the umbrella, where the handle would be, there is a mouth that opens into a big stomach. As a rule several ribbon-like streamers hang down from around the mouth. Around the edge of the umbrella there is usually a fringe of feelers.

Jellyfish eat true fish and other sea animals. They first paralyze these animals with poison darts on their feelers. Then, by using their streamers, they put the food in their mouths.

Portuguese Man-of-war

This is the life story of many kinds of jellyfish: A baby jellyfish just hatched from an egg does not look much like a grown-up jellyfish. It has no umbrella or streamers or feelers, and it is very tiny. For a while it swims about. Then it settles down on a rock and grows into a strange animal that looks like a tiny plant. After a while this little animal changes so that it appears to be a pile of little saucers at the top of a stem. Soon the saucers break apart. Each one turns over and swims away. It now looks like a grown-up jellyfish except that it may be no bigger than the head of a pin. It then grows to full size. Some kinds grow to be as big as bushel baskets.

Cows furnished Jenner with a way of preventing smallpox.

Some jellyfish have beautiful colors. Some shine at night. Some are almost transparent. Some are so soft that they collapse when they are out of water. Others are more like gristle and keep their shape. Most jellyfish live in warm water.

The Portuguese man-of-war is one of the most unusual of jellyfish. Each colorful float actually supports a whole colony of animals. (See INVERTEBRATES; LIFE THROUGH THE AGES.)

JENNER, EDWARD (1749-1823) For centuries smallpox was one of the most dreaded of all diseases. Every year thousands of people died of it. Even if smallpox did not kill a person who had it, the sores that are a part of the disease left scars on his face. Less than 200 years ago one out of every ten deaths was caused by smallpox. One out of every four people had scars, or pockmarks, from it. In most countries of the world almost no one now dies of smallpox or has pock-marked skin. Edward Jenner, a kindly English doctor, found a safe way to fight this disease.

One method of fighting smallpox had long been known. It was called inoculation. In inoculation, a little pus from a sore on the skin of someone with a mild case of smallpox was scratched into the skin of a well person. A few days later the person inoculated would have smallpox in a mild form. Having a mild form of smallpox kept one from ever having it again.

By Jenner's time inoculation was fairly common. In some ways, however, it was not good. People were not so afraid of smallpox as they had been. They were not so careful about trying to make sure that the disease did not spread.

Jenner knew that cows sometimes have a disease much like smallpox. It is called cowpox. People often caught cowpox from their cows, but it made them only slightly sick. And no one who had had cowpox, it was said, ever caught smallpox. Jenner felt sure that by giving a person cowpox he could protect him from smallpox. But he studied the problem for many years before he was ready to try out his idea.

On May 14, 1796, Jenner inoculated a healthy boy with pus from the sores of a dairymaid who had cowpox. The boy became only slightly ill. Two months later Jenner inoculated him with pus from the sores of a man with smallpox. The boy did not get the disease. In an American newspaper Jenner's experiment was reported as "Something Curious in the Medical Line."

Soon Jenner's method of inoculation with cowpox became very common. People all over the world were grateful to him for having found a safe way to protect them from smallpox. They gave him many gifts. Jenner's method came to be known as vaccination. The vaccine we use today, however, does not come from people who have cowpox. Instead it comes from cows. Great care is taken to make sure that the vaccine is pure. Since the time of Jenner, scientists have found vaccines that protect people against other diseases, too. (See DISEASE GERMS; MEDICINE; SMALLPOX.)

The jerboa hunts at night in its desert home.

JERBOA The jerboas are jumping mice. There are several kinds. But they all have long tails, long hind legs, and short front legs. Jerboas live in various parts of Africa, Asia, and eastern Europe.

The best known of the jerboas is one found in Egypt. Its front legs are so short and hard to see that it is often called the "two-legged mouse." This little jerboa looks a little like a small kangaroo, but it does not hop like a kangaroo when it is not in a hurry. Instead it walks. But when it is frightened or trying to get somewhere fast, it travels in long jumps.

The Egyptian jerboa lives in the desert. Its fur is sand-colored. Since its color matches the sand, the jerboa is not easy to see even when it walks about in the daytime. Usually it sleeps in its burrow in the daytime and comes out to hunt for food at night. It eats seeds, fruits, and insects.

This little animal can be tamed. It makes an interesting pet. (See PROTECTIVE COLORING; RODENTS.)

JERUSALEM Jerusalem is a holy city. It is holy to Christians, Mohammedans, and Jews. No other city in the world is so important to so many religions.

Jerusalem is holy to Christians because Jesus did some of his teaching here. The week before he was crucified he made a triumphal entry into the city. He had his last supper with his disciples here. He was tried, crucified, and buried here. And it was here, the Bible tells us, that he rose from the dead and ascended into heaven.

The city is holy to Mohammedans because Mohammed, they believe, also ascended into heaven here.

To the Jews it is holy because for centuries it was the center of their religion. Here Solomon built his wonderful temple.

The name of the city in Arabic means "city of peace." But Jerusalem has not always been peaceful. When Jesus was alive it was a part of the great Roman Empire. After the fall of the Roman Empire, it came under the rule of Mohammedans. The wars called the Crusades were fought to rescue this city from the Mohammedans.

Jerusalem changed hands several times during the Crusades. At the end it was

The Wailing Wall

The Dome of the Rock

A Modern Moslem

again in the hands of Mohammedans. During much of modern time it has been in the hands of the Arabs. They are Mohammedans, but Christians and Jews have been free to live there and to visit.

When the new nation of Israel was founded there was a question as to who should have Jerusalem. The new state of Israel wanted it. The Arabs wished to keep it. Its fate is not yet fully settled.

Today the old part of Jerusalem has narrow, crowded streets lined with bazaars. But the new part of the city is modern.

Christians visit the 14 "stations" which mark Christ's trip to the cross. They see the Garden of Gethsemane, where he was betrayed by Judas, the Mount of Olives, where he rose to heaven, and the Church of the Holy Sepulchre built over his tomb.

Mohammedans visit the Mohammedan temple called the Mosque of Omar. Another name for it is Dome of the Rock. Here Mohammed is believed to have ascended.

Jewish pilgrims visit the Wailing Wall. Here they pray and weep because of the destruction of Solomon's magnificent temple. (See BIBLE; CRUSADES; HOLY LAND; JESUS; JEWS; MOHAMMED.)

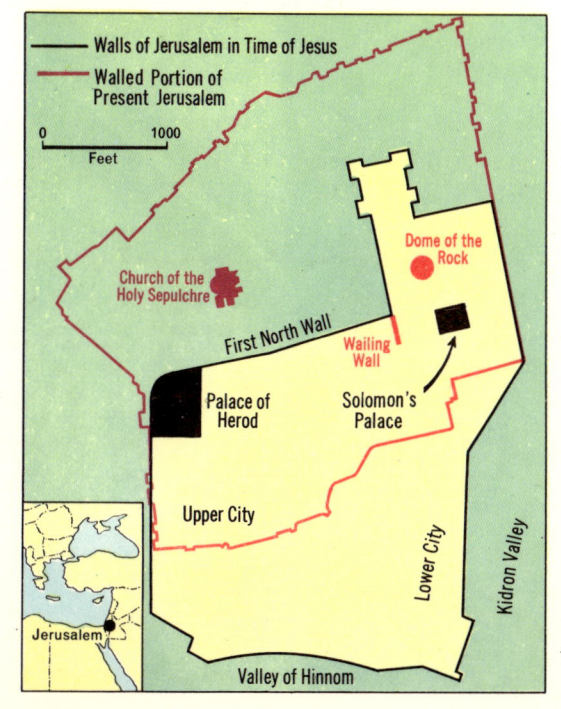

A jester often imitated his king to make him laugh.

JESTERS In the Middle Ages people did not have nearly as many ways of amusing themselves as we have now. As a way of keeping themselves entertained, the kings and queens of those days often had jesters. The jesters were supposed to say funny things and go through amusing antics.

Jesters were sometimes called court fools. Some of them were really fools. For in those days people thought that the sayings of idiots were funny. Some jesters were hunchbacks. The people of the Middle Ages thought that being deformed was funny, too. But many jesters were really clever. The rulers often asked them for their opinions. Sometimes a jester said very daring things. A king might let his jester say things which he himself wanted to say but did not dare to.

Jesters wore costumes a little like the costumes some circus clowns wear now. The costume of a jester was called "bells and motley." A cap of a special kind and shoes of a special kind were a part of the costume. There were little bells on both the cap and the shoes. "Motley" means "many-colored." The cloth of the jester's costume had patches of many colors.

A jester carried a "fool's bauble." The bauble was a rod with a fool's head at one end. A jester often made people laugh by pretending to be a king and waving his bauble as if it were his scepter. (See MIDDLE AGES.)

Joseph, Mary, and Jesus

JESUS The story of Jesus is told in the Bible. It is told in four books of the New Testament. These books are Matthew, Mark, Luke, and John.

In Bethlehem in Judea, the Bible story tells, Jesus was born to Mary, the wife of Joseph. Joseph had come with Mary to Bethlehem, the town of their forefathers, to be counted in a census ordered by the emperor of Rome. There was no room for Joseph and Mary at the inn, but they were given a place to sleep in the stable. And there, in a manger, Jesus was born.

In the fields nearby shepherds were keeping watch over their flocks. An angel appeared to them in a great blaze of light and said, "Fear not: for, behold, I bring you good tidings of great joy, which shall be to all people. For unto you is born this day in the city of David a Saviour, which is Christ the Lord." The shepherds then went to worship the baby Jesus.

A bright star shone over Bethlehem. Three wise men from the East came to Jerusalem. They saw King Herod of Judea. "Where is he that is born King of the Jews?" they asked. "For we have seen his star in the east, and are come to worship him." Herod sent them to Bethlehem. They found Jesus and gave him gifts of gold and frankincense and myrrh.

Herod did not understand what kind of king Jesus was to be. He became afraid that he would lose his own kingdom to Jesus. Perhaps he should get rid of this newborn baby. Joseph, warned in a dream

Jesus and His Twelve Disciples

of the danger, fled with Mary and Jesus to Egypt. After Herod died Joseph brought his family back to the town of Nazareth.

Jesus grew up in Nazareth. He led a quiet life. Often he helped Joseph, who was a carpenter. When he was twelve he went with Mary and Joseph to Jerusalem and talked with the learned men in the temple. They were amazed at his wisdom.

When Jesus began to teach others how to live as God wanted them to, he chose 12 disciples to go with him and help him. As he and his disciples went about, he performed many miracles. At one time he walked out on the surface of a lake in a storm to help some of his disciples who were in a boat far from shore. He made many blind people see again. He healed

Joseph and His Family Fleeing to Egypt

Jesus in the Garden of Gethsemane

others who were sick. He raised his friend Lazarus from the dead.

To make his ideas clear, he told many stories, called parables. He taught his followers how to pray, too. He gave them the Lord's Prayer.

The Jewish people had the Ten Commandments as a part of their religion. Jesus taught that these commandments should be followed. And he said "This is my commandment, That ye love one another, as I have loved you."

Jesus was always kind to the children who came to listen to him. He said, "Suffer little children to come unto me, and forbid them not, for of such is the kingdom of heaven."

Many of the Jews thought that Jesus would be a king who would rule the country. One day, as he rode into Jerusalem, crowds lined the streets. They waved palm leaves. They spread branches on the street to make a carpet. But Jesus was not to be that kind of king. He wanted only to make the people believe in, and worship, God.

Jesus had enemies. Both the Roman rulers and the Jewish priests felt that he was a danger to them. One night when Jesus went to pray in a garden, one of his disciples, Judas Iscariot, was paid 30 pieces of silver to tell Jesus' enemies where he was. Guards from the temple came to the garden and seized him. He was tried by the priests and found guilty of blasphemy. They turned him over to the Romans, who crucified him. On the cross he

Jesus Carrying the Cross

prayed for his enemies. "Father, forgive them; for they know not what they do."

Jesus was buried in a tomb cut out of a rocky hillside. Its door was a great, flat stone. Three days later, when his mother and some of his friends came to the tomb, the stone had been rolled away and the body of Jesus was gone. An angel told them that Jesus had risen from the dead. He had conquered death.

Millions of people are now Christians. They try to follow the teachings of Jesus. If everyone would follow his great commandment, the world would be a far better and happier place. (See BETHLEHEM; BIBLE; CHRISTIANITY; CHRISTMAS; HOLY LAND; JERUSALEM; PASSION PLAY; TWELVE DISCIPLES.)

Judas Betrays Jesus

JEWELRY

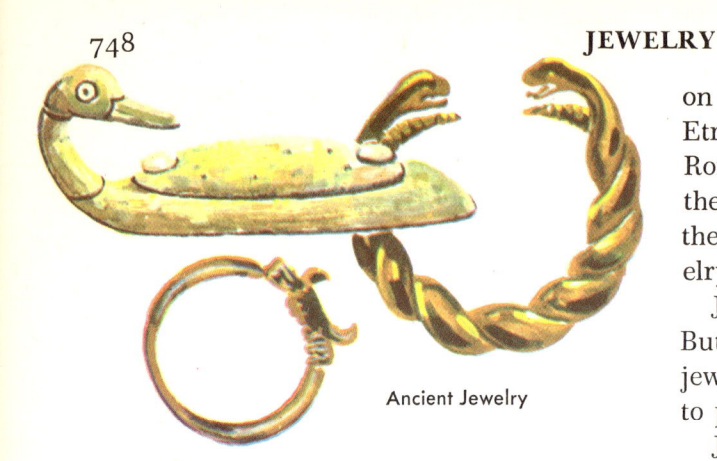

Ancient Jewelry

JEWELRY The word "jewelry" comes from "jewel," but not all jewelry has jewels set in it. Jewelry includes all such ornaments as rings, bracelets, earrings, necklaces, beads, pins, fancy combs, cuff links, and clips. Much jewelry is made of gold, silver, and platinum. But some is made of shells, wood, glass, or ivory.

The story of jewelry is as old as the story of people. No one knows of a time when mankind did not have jewelry of some sort. By the time people knew how to write there were skilled makers of jewelry. The ancient Egyptians liked color in their jewelry. They used much beautiful blue lapis lazuli and red carnelian. The Greeks, on the other hand, used few gems. The Etruscans, who lived in Italy before the Romans grew powerful, are famous for their work with gold. The Indians in both the Americas were making beautiful jewelry before the days of Columbus.

Jewelry is meant chiefly for decoration. But it serves other purposes, too. Some jewelry primitive peoples wear is supposed to protect them against evil spirits.

Jewelry is sometimes a sign of rank. Kings and queens have jeweled crowns.

Jewelry is also a form of wealth. The people of some parts of the world wear their fortunes on their necks and arms.

In early times all jewelry was made by hand. The best still is made by hand by skillful jewelers. And making jewelry is a popular hobby. But jewelry is now made by machine, too. Machine-made jewelry is often called costume jewelry.

There are fashions in jewelry just as there are in clothes. Platinum is now more fashionable than silver. Cameos, once very popular, are not often seen. But jewelry itself will probably never go out of fashion. (See DIAMONDS; GEMS.)

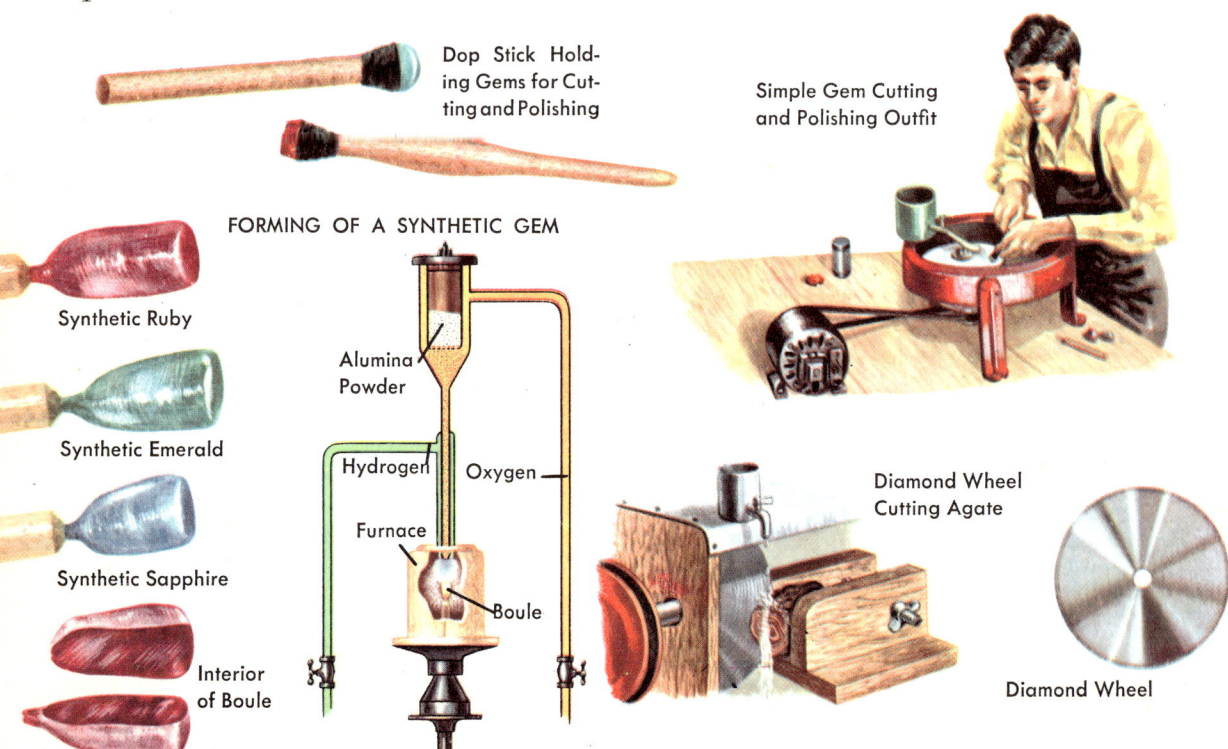

Dop Stick Holding Gems for Cutting and Polishing

Simple Gem Cutting and Polishing Outfit

Synthetic Ruby

Synthetic Emerald

Synthetic Sapphire

Interior of Boule

FORMING OF A SYNTHETIC GEM

Alumina Powder

Hydrogen

Oxygen

Furnace

Boule

Diamond Wheel Cutting Agate

Diamond Wheel

The Ten Commandments were given to Moses on tablets.

JEWS The Jewish people have a very long history. It goes back to the time nearly 4,000 years ago when they were a tribe of Hebrew herdsmen who wandered about with their flocks near the eastern end of the Mediterranean Sea. The leaders of the tribe were called patriarchs. Abraham was the first great patriarch. He was followed by Isaac and Jacob.

In Jacob's time famine in the homeland drove the Hebrews into Egypt. At first they were well treated. But in time there came to be an Egyptian ruler who treated them very badly. Among other things, he ordered that every baby boy was to be drowned. But one was saved. His name was Moses.

Moses, when he grew up, promised to lead the Hebrews back to their homeland. On their way to the "promised land," Moses gave his people the Ten Commandments. There were 12 tribes when the Hebrew people reached their promised land — the descendants of the twelve sons of Jacob. They divided the land among themselves.

The tribes were ruled by judges. But there was much trouble with peoples round about. The Hebrews decided that they could hold their own against their neighbors better if they had a king. Their kingdom reached its height under King Solomon.

After Solomon's death the kingdom broke apart into two kingdoms. Ten tribes formed the kingdom of Israel. The other two formed the kingdom of Judah.

To the east was the "land of the two great rivers." Here grew up one great empire after another. One was the Assyrian Empire. The Assyrians conquered the ten tribes of Israel and took them away as captives. No one knows what became of them. They are called the "ten lost tribes."

The empire of the Assyrians fell and the empire of the Babylonians conquered the kingdom of Judah and took its people captive. From then on the people of Judah, the Judeans, were known as the Jews. These tribes were not lost. The Babylonian Empire fell to the Persians, and the Persian king Cyrus let the Jewish captives go back to their homeland.

Then came a time when the Jews were ruled by one neighboring country after another. They won their freedom for a short while. But soon they were swallowed up in the great Roman Empire. It was in the days of Roman rule that Jesus was born. The Jews had been promised that a great religious leader would arise. But they did not accept Jesus as this leader.

The Romans made life so hard for the Jews that the Jews fought for their freedom. But they lost their fight. Their city of Jerusalem was burned, and many of them were driven out of their country.

Abraham and his people moved from place to place.

Their lot was no better when the Mohammedans, or Moslems, won western Asia. The Jews would not accept Mohammed, just as they would not accept Jesus.

From then until after World War II the Jews had no homeland. They spread into Asia, Africa, Europe, and finally into the Americas. In almost every land they reached there was prejudice against them.

When cities were growing up during the Middle Ages in Europe, the Jews were often forced to live in only one small part of the city called the ghetto. But in spite of everything many Jews became famous merchants, bankers, and scholars. Even though scattered far and wide, they managed to keep their customs and their religion.

Even in modern times the Jews have been persecuted in some lands. In Russia during the days of the czars there were occasional massacres of Jews. There were similar ones in some of the other countries of Europe. Just before World War II Hitler set out to destroy all the Jewish people of Germany. Five million were put to death.

Now there is once more a Jewish nation —the new, small country of Israel. Jews all over the world are proud that they are no longer a people without a homeland.

The first part of the Bible—the part we call the Old Testament—is the sacred book of the Jews. Their laws are in a book called the Talmud. The leaders of the Jewish churches, or synagogues, are called rabbis. The Jewish people have their own calendar. Their New Year is called Rosh Hashana and comes in either September or October. Saturday is their day of worship. The sacred writings of the Jews are in Hebrew. But in their ordinary work and play the Jews use the language of the country of which they are citizens.

Today Jews are a part of the life of many nations. They have played important roles in the history of many countries. The Jews have succeeded in spite of all their misfortunes. (See BIBLE; BIBLE STORIES; ISRAEL; TEN COMMANDMENTS.)

JOAN OF ARC

JOAN OF ARC, SAINT (1412-1431) The first part of the story of Joan of Arc reads like a fairy tale. Joan, a peasant girl who could not read or write, became the leader of the armies of France. Dressed in shining armor she led the soldiers to wonderful victories. In the great cathedral of Reims she stood at the side of the king of France when he was crowned. But there the fairy tale part stops. Joan's story does not have a happy ending.

Joan was born in Domremy, a village of northern France. Her father had a farm at the edge of the village.

In those days France was not a happy land. For nearly 100 years a war had been going on between France and England. The English and their friends, the Burgundians, held much of the northern part of the country. The prince who should have been the king of France had never been crowned. He was called the dauphin. The dauphin was a weak and selfish person. He had given away much of the land of France to get money for pleasure.

When Joan was 13 she became very religious. She often went to the village church. She went out in the fields with her father's flocks, too, so that she could be alone to think and pray. In the church and out in the fields she began to see visions of some of the saints. She heard voices, too. The voices told her to have the dauphin crowned king. She must drive out the enemies of France.

Joan made up her mind to do what the voices said that she must. Her family and the village priest tried to persuade her that she had only imagined the voices. But Joan would not give up. She was finally taken to the dauphin's court.

There one of the courtiers, it is said, thought that he would play a joke on the peasant girl. He sat on the throne. The dauphin was hidden in the crowd. When Joan came into the throne room she glanced at the throne and then turned away at once. She found the dauphin and went

Joan of Arc led the French to victory.

to kneel before him. The courtiers did not have the laugh they had planned. The dauphin began to believe that this girl might win his kingdom back for him. He put her at the head of his army. She set out for the walled city of Orléans, which the English were trying to take.

Joan wore a suit of white armor. She carried a white banner embroidered with the lilies of France. She was now 17. No one had taught her how to fight or how to lead an army. But she led the soldiers to victory at Orléans. Because of this victory she is sometimes called the Maid of Orléans. Her army won other battles, too. Finally the dauphin was crowned king.

Joan had now done what the voices had told her to do. She wanted to go home. But the king begged her to go on fighting. Soon afterward she was captured by the Burgundians. They turned her over to the English. The king of France could have rescued her. But he did not.

She was tried as a witch. The judges told her that she had never heard voices and that it was a great sin to say she had. The trial lasted for days and days. Joan would not say that she had been wrong. But the judges said that she was guilty. She was burned at the stake. As the flames rose an English soldier cried, "We have burned a saint." Nearly 500 years later she was declared Saint Joan by the Roman Catholic Church. (See FRANCE.)

JOHN BULL There is no such person as John Bull. He stands for the people of England, just as Uncle Sam stands for the people of the United States. But in his pictures he does not look at all like Uncle Sam. He is always short and stout. He wears leather breeches, high boots, and a funny flat hat. Often he has a club in one hand and a bulldog beside him. (See ENGLAND; GREAT BRITAIN; UNCLE SAM.)

JOHN DOE If a bank wanted to show people how to write a check, it might show a check signed "John Doe." John Doe is not a real name. It stands for "somebody, no one knows who," or for "anybody." Lawyers often use this name in legal papers. Everyone is supposed to know that there is no such person as John Doe.

JOLIET, LOUIS (1645-1700) A century before the American Revolution the French held part of the continent of North America. Stories reached the French governor in the New World of a giant, unexplored river to the west. Some men believed this river flowed into the Pacific. The governor organized a group of men to search for this river. The man he chose to head the group was Louis Joliet.

Joliet knew much about the wilderness. He was a fur trader who had been born in Canada. He had traveled widely over the Great Lakes region, and he could speak many of the Indian languages. He knew how to make maps.

Joliet and six other men set out in May, 1673, to find the river the Indians called the *Missi Sippi* or "Father of Waters." One member of the group was Father Marquette, a French priest who had spent many years among the Indians.

The men paddled across Lake Michigan in birchbark canoes to what is now Wisconsin. They journeyed overland till they came to the Wisconsin River. They paddled down to the broad Mississippi, and down the Mississippi as far as the Arkansas River before they turned back.

Joliet and his fellow explorers were the first white men to see the upper Mississippi River. Joliet was given land in Canada as a reward. (See MARQUETTE, JACQUES; MISSISSIPPI RIVER.)

Joliet and Marquette, with five French voyageurs, explored the Mississippi.

Commodore John Paul Jones

JONES, JOHN PAUL (1747-1792) The Revolutionary War produced the first naval hero of the United States. He was John Paul Jones. Jones was born in Scotland but came to America on his first sea voyage. He was then 12 years old. Most of his life was spent at sea, much of it fighting. One of his famous sayings—"I do not wish to have command of any ship that does not sail fast, for I intend to go in harm's way"—helps explain his success as a fighter.

During the Revolutionary War he sailed the first American man-of-war. He carried to France the news of the surrender of the British army under Burgoyne at Saratoga. The French gave to his flag the first salute ever given to an American flag.

Jones fought his most famous sea battle on the ship "Bon Homme Richard." The battle with the British ship "Serapis" had gone on for hours. At one point the captain of the "Serapis" ordered Jones to surrender. "I have not yet begun to fight" was Jones's proud reply. This reply has been a battle cry of the American navy ever since. (See U.S. ARMED FORCES.)

JUJITSU For many centuries the nobles of Japan carefully guarded the secrets of a way of fighting they called jujitsu. In Japanese, *jujitsu* means "yielding art." As a way of fighting, jujitsu means not trying to overcome an opponent's strength, but seeming to yield to it. A jujitsu fighter will allow himself to seem to be knocked down by an opponent in order to catch the opponent off balance.

Jujitsu is hand-to-hand fighting without the use of weapons. Fighters trained in jujitsu learn a great deal about the human body. They learn the location of nerves which, when struck or pressed, will cause great pain or numbness. Some of these nerves are in the ankle, the wrist, the upper arm, and the side of the neck. Jujitsu fighters also learn how to get an opponent off balance and throw him to the floor with great force.

A small man who knows jujitsu can easily defeat a larger and stronger man. If the larger man rushes him, the smaller man can fall backwards and pull the big man down after him. Then he can get a hold on the larger man that will hurt or disable him.

Jujitsu fighters must be quick and skilful. They must be in good physical condi-

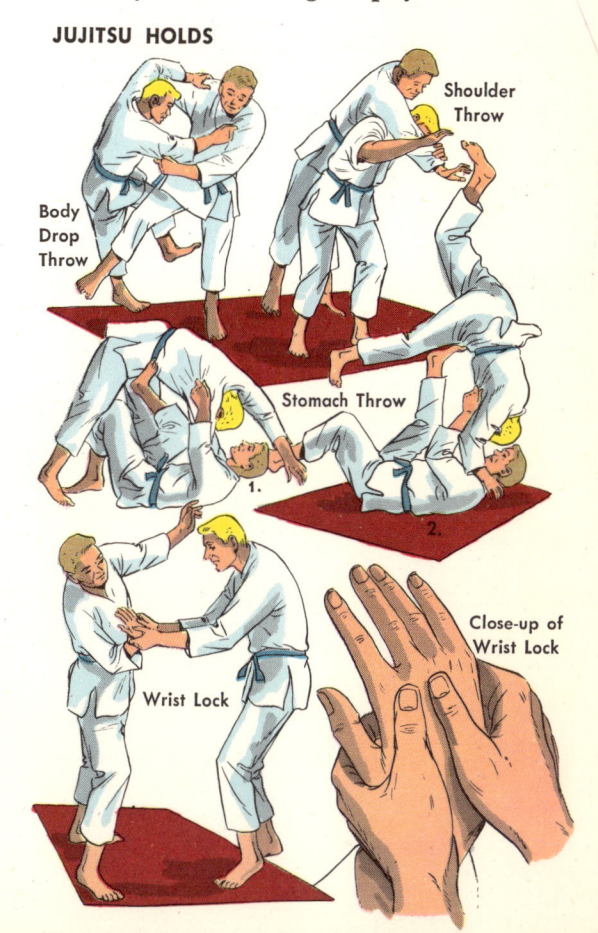

JUJITSU HOLDS

Body Drop Throw

Shoulder Throw

Stomach Throw

Wrist Lock

Close-up of Wrist Lock

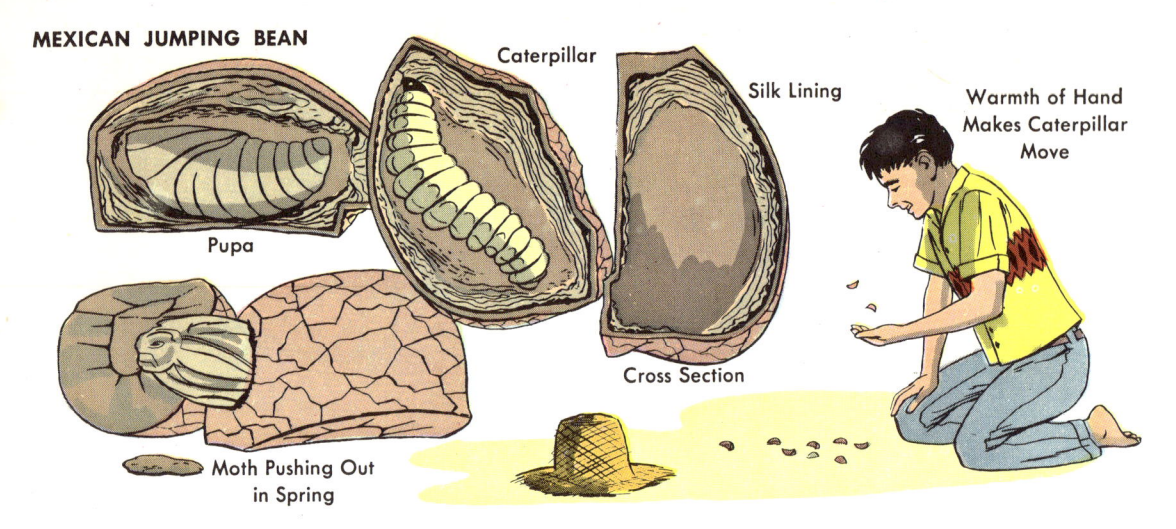

tion. They must know how to fall without hurting themselves.

Today jujitsu is no longer a secret of the Japanese. It is used in many countries of the world as a means of self-defense. Millions of American soldiers and marines were taught how to defend themselves with jujitsu during World War II. Jujitsu is also a regular part of the training of policemen and of F.B.I. agents.

JUMPING BEANS The seeds called jumping beans come from a plant which grows in Mexico. Of course, a jumping bean would not jump if it were only a seed. It is a seed which has become a nursery for a baby moth. The baby moth puts the jump in the bean.

This is the way a seed is made into a nursery: A female moth lays an egg in the seed when it is just forming. The seed develops around the egg. The plant stores up food for the baby plant in the seed. But the baby plant never gets the food. The moth egg hatches into a tiny caterpillar. It begins at once to eat and grow. It eats all the food in the seed and even the baby plant. Only the seed coat is left. It is like a shell around the caterpillar.

The caterpillar then lines its "shell" with silk. As it spins the silk it moves from side to side and makes the bean jump. For several months the little caterpillar lives inside the seed. During those months the bean may stop jumping. But the heat from a person's hand may make the insect move and thus make the bean jump again.

When the caterpillar is about to spin its cocoon, it cuts almost through one side of the bean. The moth that comes from the cocoon has no trouble pushing its way out.

There are games in which jumping beans are used. One company has sold more than a million beans for use in these games. (See BUTTERFLIES AND MOTHS; SEEDS.)

JUNGLES Most boys and girls of today know the word "jungle." For they have read the story of Mowgli in Kipling's *Jungle Book*. Mowgli's jungle was in India, but there are jungles in other parts of the world, too. There are jungles in southeastern Asia and on the islands near by. There are jungles in Central America, along the Amazon River in South America, and in vast areas in the middle of Africa.

A jungle is a tangled growth of trees and other wild plants. Plants need water, warmth, and sunshine. It is easy to understand, then, why the world's jungles are in rainy lands near the equator. Jungles are often called "tropical forests."

In a jungle the plants are always fighting for sunlight. Some of them win the fight by growing very tall and slender. Some of them spread their leaves out flat to catch

JUNGLES

the light. Many of the plants of a jungle perch high on the branches of trees. Many other plants are vines. A jungle tree may not fall even if it is cut clear through near the ground. Vines may hold it in place.

Many jungle plants have gorgeous flowers. Beautiful orchids come from the jungles. Some jungle plants are poisonous. Many of the poisons we use in killing insects come from jungle plants. The Indians that live near the Amazon in South America often use poisoned arrows in hunting. The poison comes from a jungle vine.

Almost every jungle has some big "cats" in it. Tigers and leopards, for instance, are found in the jungles of India. Every jungle has its monkeys and bats, too. But mammals are not the most common jungle animals. There are far more birds, reptiles, and insects. The ancestor of all our chickens today was the jungle fowl of India. Parrots are jungle birds. There are many snakes and lizards among the trees and many alligators or crocodiles in the rivers that flow through jungles. A "branch" hanging down from a tree may be a big snake looking for food. A "log" in a river may be a sleepy crocodile.

A jungle is a paradise for insects. Insects are the worst enemies of jungle explorers, for some of the insects carry disease. Others are merely a nuisance. There are many kinds of ants in jungles. If a garden is growing in a bit of cleared land there, the whole garden may be ruined in a single night by an invasion of army ants.

Plants grow thick along jungle trails.

Even though there are plants on every side in a jungle, it is not easy for a person to find food there. Anyone might think jungle living would be as easy as living on an island in the South Seas, where coconuts and breadfruit fall from the trees. But few plants of the jungle bear anything good to eat. A person lost in a jungle might have to eat locusts, lizards, and caterpillars to keep from starving.

Parts of the jungles have been conquered. Some parts have been turned into plantations. Some have been changed into pasture land. Even cities have been built in the jungles. But keeping a plantation or a pasture or even a city from going back to jungle means a constant fight. Hidden away in the jungles of the world there are ruins of many cities of yesterday. (See AMAZON RIVER; ANGKOR; EPIPHYTES; MAYAS; ORCHIDS.)

JUNGLE LIFE

Bat
Leopard
Tiger
Orchid

There are about 225 different kinds of monkeys living in the many jungles of the world.

British courts still keep ancient traditions.

JUSTICE Often Justice is shown as a goddess blindfolded and holding a balance. It is easy to see why Justice is holding scales. No one can be just in settling a question unless he hears both sides of it and weighs carefully what has been said on each side. It is not so easy to see why Justice is blindfolded. Perhaps the idea is that the blindfold helps insure complete fairness to both sides in a legal dispute.

Ever since there have been people on the earth some have thought that they were treated unfairly by others. Ever since there have been laws people have been accused of breaking the laws. For thousands of years, therefore, ways of meting out justice have been needed.

In the days when most people lived in tribes, the leader of the tribe was usually the one who settled disputes. After there were kings, the kings were often called on to deal out justice. Many stories are told of how cleverly some of the early rulers decided who was right in a dispute.

One of these stories is about how King Solomon settled a question about a child. Two women came before him with a baby boy. Each woman claimed that the boy was hers. After he had heard their claims, Solomon sent for a sword. "Cut the child in two," said Solomon, "and give half to each woman." One of the women then begged Solomon not to cut the baby in two. "I will give him up," she said. "I would far rather give him up than have him hurt."

Solomon now knew that this woman was the child's mother and gave the boy to her.

More than a few rulers became famous for their fairness. The words "the Just" were often added to their names.

Some of the ways of meting out justice during the Middle Ages seem very peculiar today. If a person was accused of some misdoing, he might defend himself in several ways. Fighting a duel was one way. If he won, he was considered innocent. Trial by ordeal was another way. The accused man might have his arms and feet bound and be thrown into a river. If the river "refused to accept him" and he floated, he was guilty. If he sank, he was innocent. Trial by evidence was a third way. A person who was accused brought in people to testify that he was a good man. If he could bring in enough people, and if the people praised him enough, he was called innocent.

Today in all civilized countries there are courts for settling disputes. Judges are in charge of the courts. In many of these courts juries decide whether the accused person is guilty or innocent. Right of trial by jury is one of the rights the founders of the United States promised every American. A trial jury is a group of 12 or more people who decide whether the accused person is guilty or not.

Although trial by jury is the modern way of settling disputes, it is not new. The English people won the right of trial by jury in 1215 when their King John signed the Magna Carta. Some questions were settled by jury trials even in ancient Greece.

In a jury trial the judge sees to it that the trial is fair. If the jury decides that the accused person is guilty, the judge decides what the punishment will be. During the trial both sides have lawyers to argue for them. Even a very poor person who is accused of some misdoing is given a lawyer to defend him. Deciding a case may not be at all easy. But our courts are set up to give justice to all. (See LAWS; MAGNA CARTA; U. S. CONSTITUTION.)

K • KANGAROO 757

The letter *K* can be traced back to a letter in the Phoenician alphabet—a letter which the Phoenicians wrote in two ways (ᚺ Ж). Some scholars think that the letter had its beginning in Egyptian writing as the picture of a certain plant. One of the ways the Phoenicians wrote the letter does look a little like a bush. When the Greeks borrowed the letter for their alphabet, they wrote it in this way: K . The Romans did not change it, and it came down to us from them.

K stands for only one sound—the sound it has in *kite* and *kitten*. In *knee*, *knight*, and some other words it is silent.

KALEIDOSCOPE (ka LY da skope) A kaleidoscope is a toy made with mirrors. Two long, narrow mirrors, fastened together lengthwise to form a V, are fitted into a tube. A round piece of cardboard or metal across one end of the tube has a peephole at the center. At the other end of the tube there is an object box made of two round pieces of glass with a little space between them. In the space there are bits of colored paper, glass, or plastic.

A person turns the kaleidoscope slowly as he looks through it. The bits of colored material fall into one position after another. In each position they are reflected in the mirrors, and the reflections are reflected back and forth so that they make beautiful patterns. No two patterns are ever exactly alike.

Kaleidoscope

Color Patterns

KANGAROO Many animals of Australia carry their babies in pouches. The kangaroo is one of these pouched animals.

A kangaroo uses its strong hind legs in making leaps of as much as 25 feet. It is good that a kangaroo can cover ground fast. This animal eats grass and other plants. It lives on the dry plains of Australia, where plant food is not easy to find. Of course, being able to go fast also helps a kangaroo escape from its enemies.

A baby kangaroo just born looks like a small red grub. It would not have a chance of growing up if it did not have its mother's pouch to crawl into.

Even after a baby kangaroo is able to hop about by itself, it often hops back into its mother's pouch if it is frightened. It is fun to wonder how a little kangaroo in its mother's pouch feels when its mother takes a 25-foot leap. (See AUSTRALIA; KOALA; POUCHED MAMMALS.)

KANSAS The name Kansas comes from an Indian word, *Kansa*, said to mean "people of the south wind." Kansas is nicknamed the "Sunflower State." Early settlers found many sunflowers there.

Kansas lies halfway between the east coast and the west coast of the United States. Many pioneers crossed the Kansas country in the days of the Oregon and Santa Fe trails. Today many people travel the paved highways, railways, and air lines that cross Kansas linking East and West. Kansas is one of the larger, rather thinly settled states.

Early American explorers said that the Kansas country was a "useless waste of sand." No wonder many pioneers in the 1840's and 1850's merely crossed the Kansas prairies seeking rich land and gold farther west. A few stopped to settle in eastern Kansas, which receives more rain and snow than the western part. The stirring question of slavery later brought more settlers. Some wanted Kansas to have only free labor. Others, from the South, brought their slaves. There was a struggle. Those against slave labor won. Kansas joined the Union in 1861 as a free state. Topeka became the capital.

The early settlers used the Kansas prairies chiefly for pasturing longhorn cattle. In the 1860's railroad lines pushed farther west through the state. Kansas and Texas cowboys drove herds of longhorn cattle northward over the "Long Trail" to the railroads. They shipped the cattle to eastern markets from little shipping towns along the rail line called "cow towns." Cowboys had lively times in such cow towns as Abilene and Dodge City.

The railroads attracted settlers by offering them cheap land. The roads needed farm products to fill their freight cars.

Kansas farmers have to contend with dry years, prairie fires, and tornadoes. But more of the people of Kansas make a living by farming than by any other kind of work. To overcome some of their handicaps, Kansas farmers do terracing and contour plowing. Belts of trees, called shelter belts, are planted to help keep water on the farmlands. Water is pumped from wells to irrigate the land.

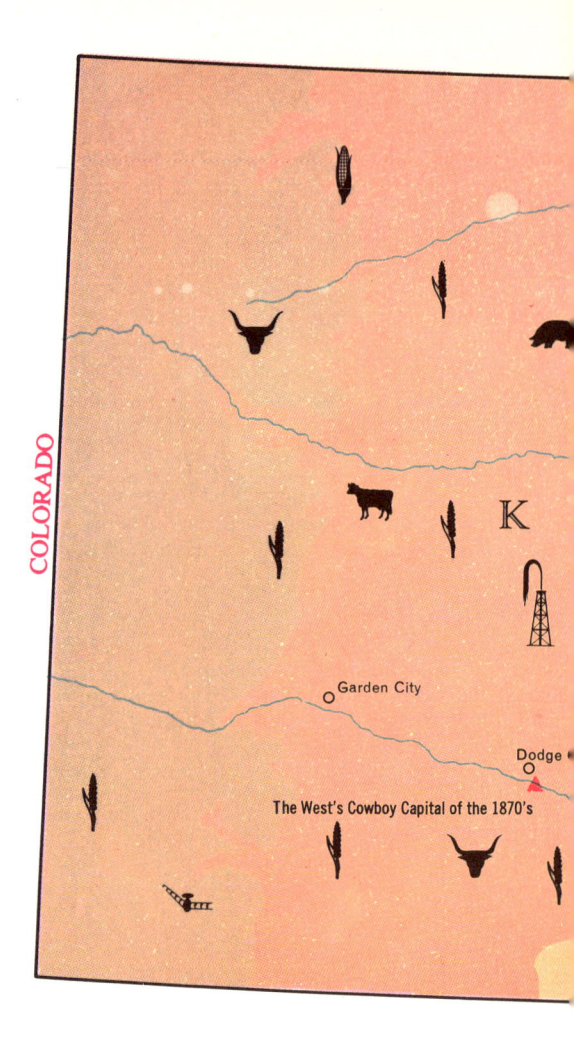

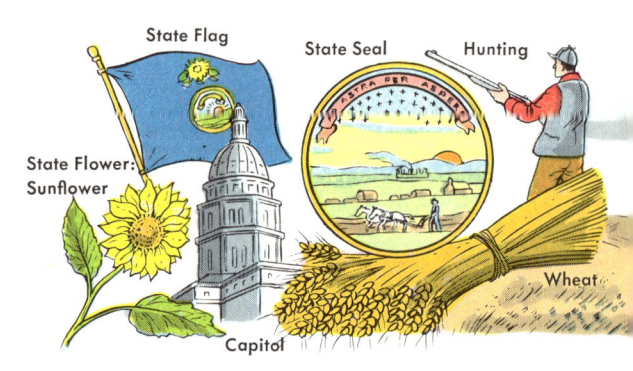

In the rainier eastern regions Kansas farmers do corn-and-livestock farming. In the drier western section they raise bumper crops of wheat. Wheat is the big money crop. Kansas ranks first in wheat growing

KANSAS

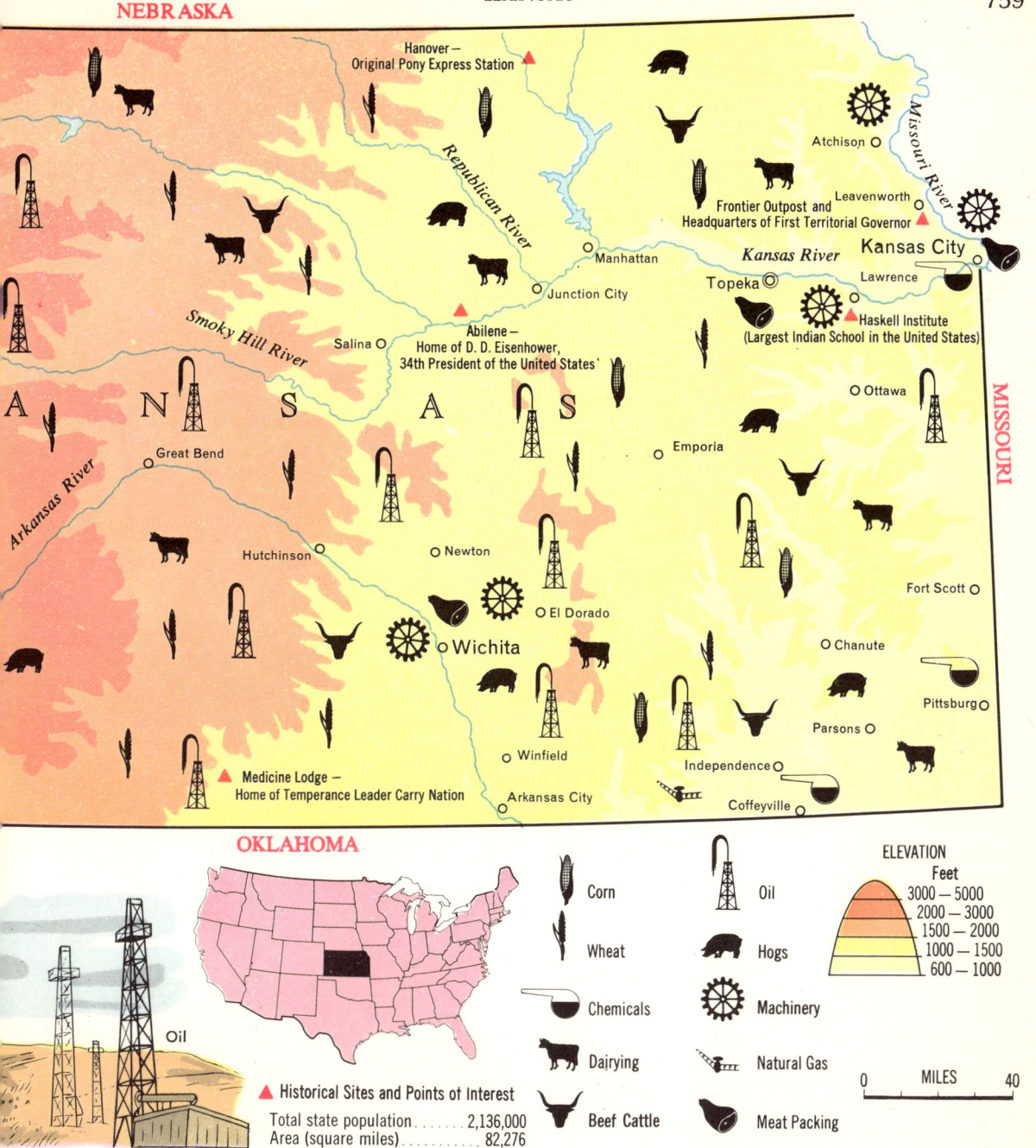

and in flour milling. No wonder it is called "The Bread Basket of America." In western Kansas there are also many cattle ranches where livestock feed on the dry grasses of the plains. Some of these ranches cover 50,000 acres. The ranchers use part of their land for raising crops to help fatten their animals.

Wichita and Kansas City are the largest trade and manufacturing centers of the state. Each has more than 100,000 people. Wichita has grown rapidly since the discovery of petroleum in Kansas. Much of its work depends on petroleum, but flour milling is its most important industry. It was one of the first cities to have airplane factories. Kansas City has large stockyards and meat-packing plants. Kansas is a state with a promising future. (See CATTLE; FLOUR; WHEAT.)

KENTUCKY

KENTUCKY The name Kentucky comes from an Indian word *ken-tah-ten*. No one is sure of the meaning of the Indian word. Some say that it means "meadowland." Others say that it means "land of tomorrow." Kentucky's nickname, "Bluegrass State," comes from the bluegrass that grows in the north-central part of the state.

For years after the 13 American colonies were founded, the rugged Appalachian Mountains kept settlers from moving westward. But not long before the Revolution explorers found their way through the Cumberland Gap into the region that is now Kentucky. Thomas Walker was the first to reach Kentucky. Some years later Daniel Boone explored the Kentucky country. He reported that it was beautiful, fertile, and full of game. In 1774, just two years before the Declaration of Independence was signed, James Harrod and a band with him made the first settlement in Kentucky. Their new home was called Harrodsburg. Later in the same year Boone and a few pioneers settled Boonesborough.

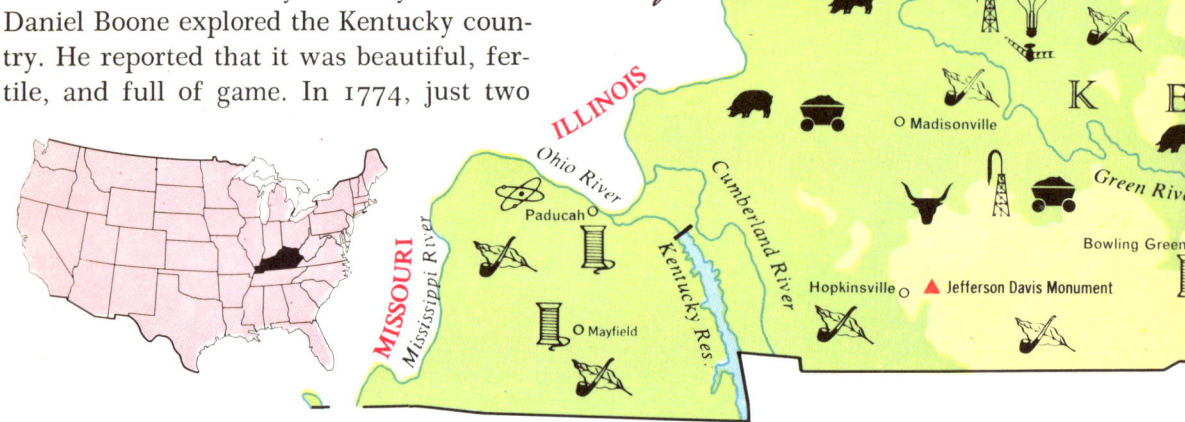

Soon thousands of settlers poured through the Gap to live in Kentucky. The settlers built log forts surrounded by high log walls to protect them from the Indians. The frontiersmen were called "long knives" and "the tall men of Kentucky." They raised horses on the bluegrass pastures. Hemp was their first money crop but tobacco soon took its place. They grew corn, too, and fed hogs and cattle.

Kentucky became a state in 1792. It was the 15th state to join the Union—the very first of the pioneer states west of the Appalachians. Later many settlers came down the Ohio River in steamboats to settle in Kentucky.

Today the bluegrass region of Kentucky is noted for its horse farms, on which are raised some of the finest race horses in the world. Every year the Kentucky Derby, a very famous race, draws thousands of visitors to Churchill Downs near Louisville. Many of the farms in the bluegrass region now raise cattle, too. Corn and tobacco are still important crops in Kentucky.

Kentucky has rich coal deposits, and much coal is mined. With both coal and iron ore at hand, Ashland was the first iron and steel center west of the Appalachians. Louisville, Kentucky's largest city, is a great market for tobacco, cigarettes, and whiskey. It manufactures farm machinery and electrical appliances, and tans leather. Among Kentucky's other cities are Coving-

KENTUCKY

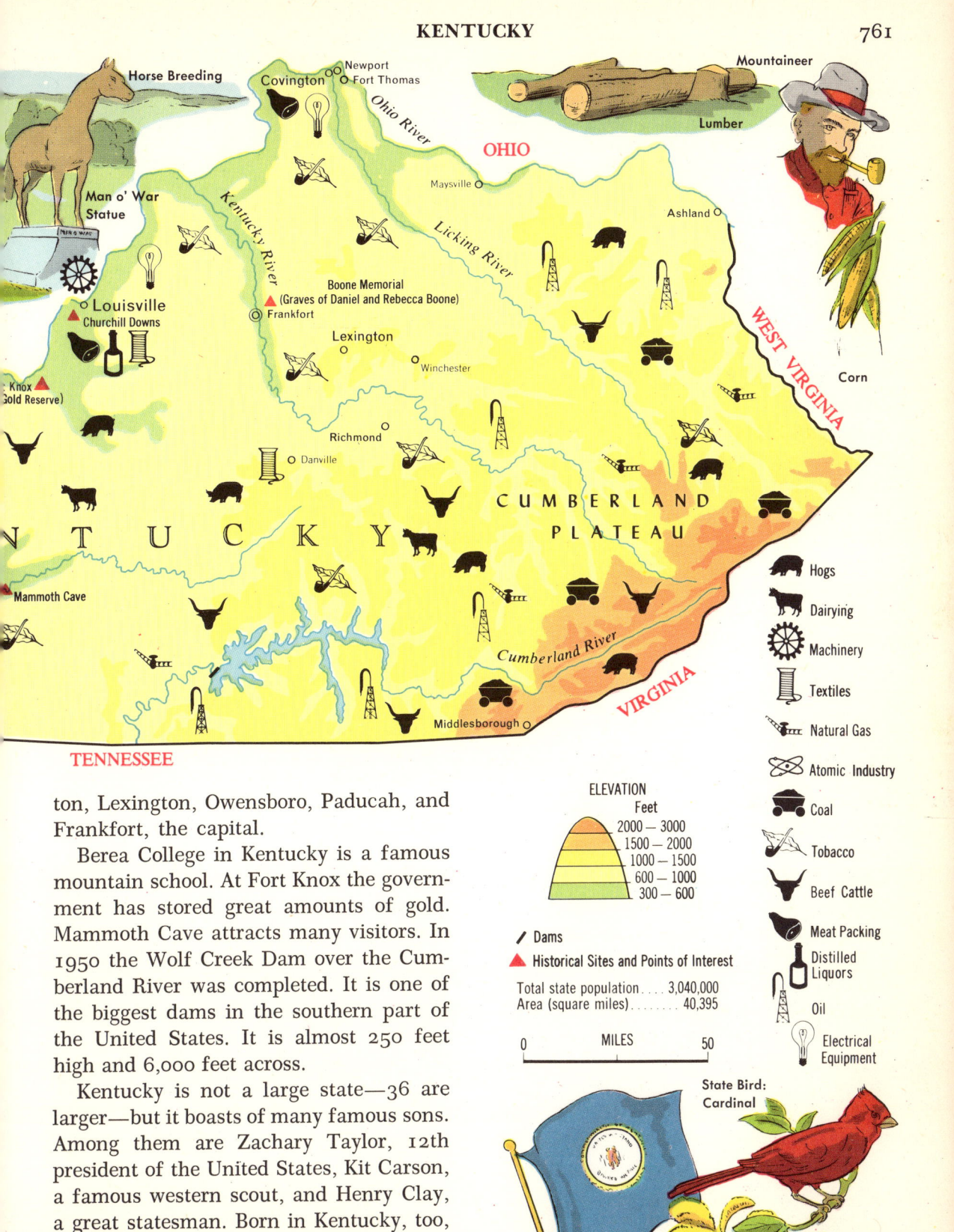

ton, Lexington, Owensboro, Paducah, and Frankfort, the capital.

Berea College in Kentucky is a famous mountain school. At Fort Knox the government has stored great amounts of gold. Mammoth Cave attracts many visitors. In 1950 the Wolf Creek Dam over the Cumberland River was completed. It is one of the biggest dams in the southern part of the United States. It is almost 250 feet high and 6,000 feet across.

Kentucky is not a large state—36 are larger—but it boasts of many famous sons. Among them are Zachary Taylor, 12th president of the United States, Kit Carson, a famous western scout, and Henry Clay, a great statesman. Born in Kentucky, too, were the leaders of both the North and the South in the War between the States—Abraham Lincoln and Jefferson Davis.

The kinkajou's large eyes help him in night hunting.

KINKAJOU The kinkajou is sometimes called the "honey bear." Another name for it is "night monkey." Neither of these names is good, for this little animal is neither a bear nor a monkey. It is a cousin of the raccoon. But it does not have the raccoon's black mask.

As it sits up, a kinkajou looks a little like a small bear except for its long tail. It can hang upside down by curling this long tail around branches. In zoos many visitors like to watch the kinkajous hang head down as they eat.

Kinkajous are found in the forests of South America, Central America, and Mexico. In their forest homes they sleep during the day. At night they travel through the trees in groups like monkeys as they hunt for food. One can easily see how they get the name of night monkeys. Of course, they are also like many monkeys in being able to hang by their tails.

These little animals make good pets. But they need a great deal of food. To a kinkajou three or four big bananas are no more than a light lunch.

KIPLING, RUDYARD (1865-1936) Born in Bombay, India, Rudyard Kipling was the son of an art teacher from England. From native nurses Kipling heard the stories of jungle animals—stories the Indian people told their own children.

When Kipling was six years old, he was sent to England to be educated. He became ill, however, and did not go to school until five years later. When he was ready to go to college, his parents told him he might do that or return to India. He decided to go to Lahore, India, where his father was then director of a museum.

In Lahore Kipling went to work for a newspaper. He wrote a number of poems and short stories which appeared in the paper. They were later published in two books. In 1887 he went to Allahabad to work on a newspaper there. Most of his spare time he spent in writing stories.

By the time he was 26 years old he was already a famous author. On a visit to England he met and married an American girl. With his new wife he went to live in Brattleboro, Vt., his wife's home.

For his own children he wrote *The Jungle Book*, *The Second Jungle Book*, and

KIPLING STORIES

The Jungle Book

"How the Elephant Got His Trunk"

"Rikki-Tikki-Tavi"

TYPES OF KITES — Box Kite, Plain Kite, Chinese Kite

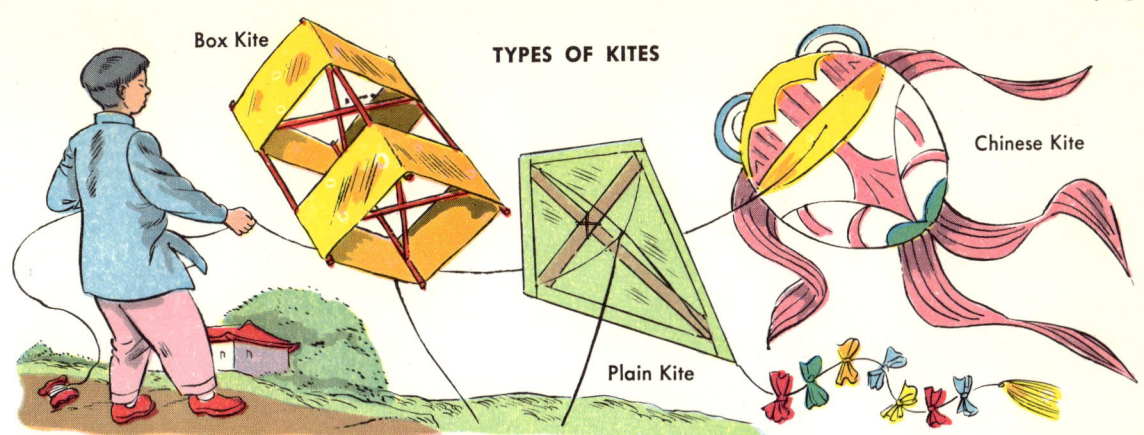

Just So Stories. While living in Vermont he also wrote *Captains Courageous*, a story of a rich boy's experiences with a crew of New England fishermen.

After a few years in America Kipling took his family to England, where he lived the rest of his life. There he wrote other stories, among them *Stalky & Co.* and *Puck of Pook's Hill*. The little boy called Beetle in *Stalky & Co.* is really Kipling. The story tells about the author's schooldays. (See ENGLISH WRITERS.)

KITES Boys and girls have flown kites as toys for many years. No one knows who invented the kite. We do know that a flat kite had been used in China for more than 2,000 years. Kites have meant a great deal to the people of China, Japan, and Korea. Not only boys and girls but also grown people fly kites for fun there. Some of their kites, like the Chinese kite in the picture, are gaily decorated. The Chinese enjoyed flying kites so much that the ninth day of their ninth month was made Kites' Day and is still a great holiday.

But kites have been much used for other things besides toys. The ancient Chinese flew kites above their houses to drive evil spirits away. Armies formerly used kites in sending signals from one place to another. Big suspension bridges have been started from lines carried across deep valleys by kites. And weather bureaus have sent weather instruments high into the air by using kites.

A kite played an important part in one very famous experiment. Benjamin Franklin used a kite in finding out that lightning is a great spark of electricity.

The United States Weather Bureau succeeded in making kites carry weather instruments more than four miles above the earth. To reach such great heights they used a train made up of several kites.

The picture shows three kinds of kites. Ordinary flat kites have to have tails. The tail weighs down the lower end and helps keep the kite from taking a nose dive. Box kites do not need tails. The Chinese kite in the picture has streamers.

Strings are attached to kites so as to hold them at a slant. The wind pushes against the undersurface and at the same time rushes around the edges of the kite and drags some of the air from the upper side. It creates what scientists call a partial vacuum there. The push of the air on the underside is much greater than the push on the upper side and the kite is held in the air. It is held up in the same way that an airplane is held up. The difference is that an airplane has to keep moving rapidly through the air to make the pressure above and below its wings different, while a kite depends on the wind to do this.

Although wind is needed for kite flying, the best kite-flying days are not the days when there are strong winds. The best days are those with a gentle breeze. (See AIRPLANES; FRANKLIN, BENJAMIN; U. S. WEATHER BUREAU.)

Squires dress a knight while a page leads up his horse.

KNIGHTHOOD One part of the Middle Ages is called the Age of Chivalry. This was the time when brave knights fought for the honor of God and of their lords and for the protection of the weak.

No one could become a knight unless he was wellborn. His family had to be noble and own land. Even the younger sons of noble families usually could not be knights.

A boy who wished to be a knight had to begin his training very early. When he was only seven or eight he became a page in the service of some lord. A few years later he became a squire. As a page or squire he waited upon his master. He served him at table, ran his errands, and was at hand to help him in every battle or tournament. In his free time he practiced many sports, some of them dangerous. He learned to handle the weapons the knights used—the stout swords and long lances.

Some squires were made knights on the battlefield because of some brave deed. They were called "knights of the sword." But many squires became knights in a long ceremony in the castle of their lord. This ceremony started with a bath of purification. The knights who gained their knighthood in such a ceremony were called "knights of the bath."

In this ceremony the squire, or candidate, was dressed in a pure-white tunic, a red robe, and a black cloak. The white of the tunic stood for purity. Every knight was supposed to be pure in thought and deed. The red stood for blood. A knight was expected to be ready to shed his blood in a good cause. The black of the cloak stood for death. A knight had to be ready to face death in fighting for the right.

Knights in Battle

Dressed in his knightly robes the candidate fasted for a day. In the evening he went to church. The vigil there lasted all night. In the morning, at the end of a solemn church service, the youth went to the altar with his sword hanging around his neck. The priest blessed the sword.

The youth then turned to his lord, who was seated near by. "Why," the lord asked, "do you desire to enter the order?" The candidate gave his answer, vowing to do honor to knighthood. His answer was accepted. Then knights or ladies dressed him in a suit of armor and gave him spurs of gold. "Win his spurs" was another way of saying "become a knight." The lord then rose and struck the youth three times lightly on the shoulders with a sword. As he did so he said, "In the name of God, St. Michael, and St. George, I dub thee knight."

The young knight then received a lance, a helmet, and a horse. He mounted his horse, brandished his lance, and rode away.

Once he was a knight, the youth could take part in tournaments. Tournaments were mock battles which helped to keep knights in good fighting trim. Often they were gay festivals.

Tournaments were held by kings and noblemen to celebrate such things as the visit of a king, the wedding of some great lord, or the making of a new knight. Heralds went far and wide to invite knights. Along with the knights came fortune tellers, acrobats, troubadours, and actors. Lords and ladies in gorgeous costumes came as an audience. Almost every knight carried on his helmet or lance or shield a scarf or ribbon from his chosen lady.

Some of the contests were between only two knights. They were called "jousts" (JUSTS) or "tilts." But there was always a tourney, too. It was a contest in which many knights fought on each side.

To live up to his vows a knight had to be a gentleman, a hero, and a saint. Galahad in the story of the Knights of the Round Table was the example of all that a knight should be. Of course, most knights fell short of this ideal. But trying to live up to it brought about great good. And no better stories have ever been written than some of the stories of knights and their brave deeds. (See ARTHUR; MIDDLE AGES.)

Knight Receiving his Sword from a Lady

Sounding the Trumpet for a Tournament

Hand to Hand Combat of Knights

KNITTING STITCHES: Rib, Knit, Position, Cable, Purl

KNITTING Thousands of years ago our ancestors learned to weave yarn into cloth. Knitting is much newer. But it is not new. It is several hundred years old. In weaving there are up-and-down threads and cross threads. Knitting can be done with a single thread.

In knitting, yarn is looped through loops. Knitted materials are looser and more stretchy than woven materials. But they do not keep their shape as well.

The first knitting we know about was done by fishermen's wives in Scotland. They knitted caps for their husbands. Of course, they did their knitting by hand. The finest knitted suits and sweaters and baby clothes are still knitted by hand. They are knitted on knitting needles. But most knitting is now done by machine.

The knitting machine was invented in England in the days of Queen Elizabeth I. The inventor was William Lee. One story is that he invented the machine because the girl he loved spent too much time knitting instead of talking to him. Lee gave the Queen a pair of silk stockings he had knitted on his machine. She was pleased, but she would not give Lee a patent on the machine. She was afraid it would throw many knitters out of work.

Knitting machines can knit yarn of many kinds. Wool, silk, rayon, and nylon are the yarns most used. All hosiery is knitted. Hosiery is knitted in the shape it is to be. So are many suits and sweaters. But yard goods also can be knitted and then cut and sewed into clothing. Tricot and jersey are both knitted materials.

KNIVES, FORKS, AND SPOONS In early times even kings and queens ate with their fingers. Later, people began eating with spoons. Many years later they started using knives and forks.

The first spoons meant for use at a table were made out of expensive metals such as gold, bronze, and silver. Because spoons were not useful in eating all kinds of food, forks were invented.

The first forks had only two prongs. They were designed by the wife of an Italian nobleman about 1100. Forks soon became common in Italy. Then knives for use at table became common, too. The use of knives and forks spread far and wide from Italy. But in some countries, such as China and Japan, knives and forks never came to be common tools for eating. Most Chinese and Japanese still use chopsticks.

Silver and stainless steel are the metals now most popular for "table silver." There are many beautiful patterns. Of course, knives, forks, and spoons of many sizes and shapes are found in the kitchen, too.

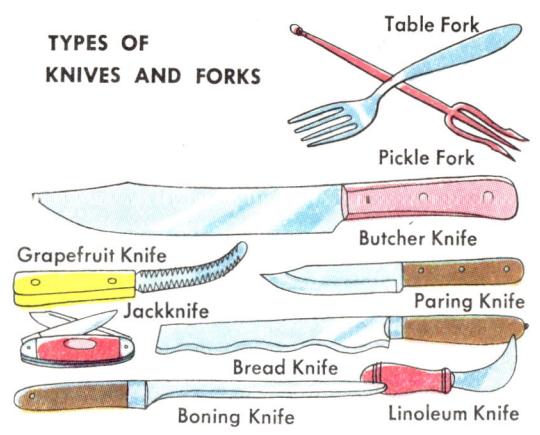

TYPES OF KNIVES AND FORKS: Table Fork, Pickle Fork, Butcher Knife, Grapefruit Knife, Paring Knife, Jackknife, Bread Knife, Boning Knife, Linoleum Knife

KNOTS By the time he starts to school almost every child can tie his own shoestrings. He may tie them in a hard knot. It may be a granny knot or a square knot. But probably he has learned to tie them in a bowknot instead. A bowknot is easier to untie than a hard knot.

We all tie at least a few knots. Some people do kinds of work that make them tie a great many. Among these people are tai-

KNOTS

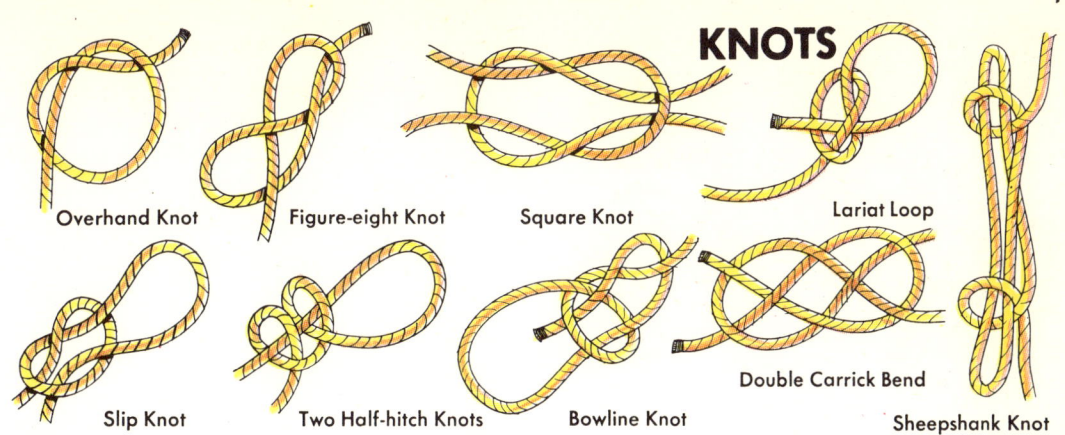

Overhand Knot, Figure-eight Knot, Square Knot, Lariat Loop, Slip Knot, Two Half-hitch Knots, Bowline Knot, Double Carrick Bend, Sheepshank Knot

lors, sailors, fishermen, lumbermen, cowboys, rugmakers, and surgeons.

There are many kinds of knots. The overhand knot is the simplest of them. It is used to keep the end of a rope from unraveling. A figure-eight at the end of a rope will keep the rope from sliding through a pulley. The bowline, which is sometimes called the king of knots, is very useful when something heavy has to be lifted or lowered with a rope. A double carrick bend is a good way of securely tying two ropes together to make a longer one. A sheepshank is a way of shortening a rope without cutting it.

Some knots are slipknots; the loop, or "eye," gets smaller when the free end of the rope is pulled. The lariat loop is a slipknot very useful to cowboys. Hitch knots are especially useful for tying up boats, horses, or cows.

Boy Scouts learn to tie many kinds of knots. They need to know how to tie knots when they go camping.

KOALA Teddy bears have been common stuffed toys for many years. They look like koalas. And no wonder! The maker of the first teddy bear got the idea from seeing a stuffed koala. Koalas are found only in the woods of Australia.

These little animals are not bears. They are much closer relatives of the kangaroo. They carry their babies in pouches in the same way kangaroos do.

Koalas have thick, soft fur. With their big fuzzy ears, little eyes, and noses that look false, they are rather comical-looking creatures. They spend most of the daytime asleep high up in trees.

Usually only one koala baby is born at a time. A koala baby when it is first born is very tiny. It could easily be put in a thimble. It could not possibly live to grow up if its mother did not have a safe place for it. The baby stays in its mother's pouch about six months. Then for three months

The koala feeds on eucalyptus leaves.

or more it rides on its mother's back as she climbs through the trees.

Their fur shows that koalas are mammals. Baby koalas get milk from their mothers just as all mammal babies do. After they are grown, koalas normally eat nothing but the leaves of certain eucalyptus trees. Zoos outside Australia seldom have koalas because of the difficulty of getting the right food for them. (See AUSTRALIA; POUCHED MAMMALS.)

KOREA

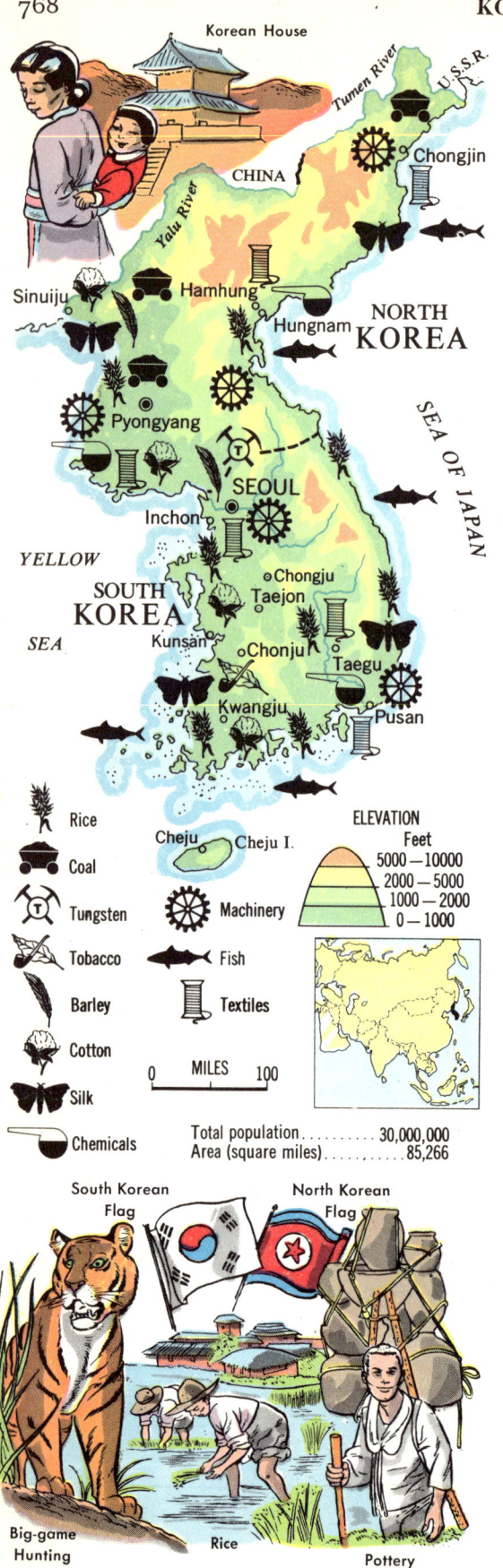

KOREA Stretching southward in eastern Asia, along the Yellow Sea, there is a peninsula called the Korean Peninsula. The country of Korea filled this mountainous peninsula for more than 1,250 years. In 1948 the country was divided into North Korea and South Korea. But this division may not be lasting.

On a map of huge Asia, Korea looks very small. Actually it is almost exactly the size of Minnesota. But it is much more crowded. About 30,000,000 people live in it. More than two-thirds of them live in South Korea, which is quite a bit smaller in area than North Korea.

Among the riches of Korea as a whole are iron, coal, forests, and farmland. Most Koreans are farmers. But many work in factories, mines, and forests. Most of the farmland is in South Korea. The chief mining district is in North Korea.

The Koreans were highly civilized 2,000 years ago. They learned to write in very early times. Korea is known to its people as Chosen. This name means "Land of Morning Calm." But modern times have not been calm times in Chosen. First China and then Japan conquered and ruled it.

At the end of World War II, defeated Japan lost Korea. By 1948, Koreans had worked out a good plan for governing their newly freed country. But communists in the north set up a separate government for North Korea. So only South Korea was left in the new free republic.

In 1950, people of North Korea tried to conquer South Korea. Then the United Nations sent troops to help protect the South Koreans. In turn, communist China sent troops to help conquer South Korea. Great damage was done and many lives were lost before the fighting was stopped.

Now South Korea has many new factories, power plants, and other things built with the aid of money and helpers sent from many lands. South Koreans are making much progress in doing things to help their new free republic and its people.

THE GOLDEN BOOK ENCYCLOPEDIA
CONTAINS THE FOLLOWING VOLUMES

I	Aardvark to Army	IX	Labor Day to Matches
II	Arthur to Blood	X	Mathematics to Natural Gas
III	Boats to Cereals	XI	Navy to Parasites
IV	Chalk to Czechoslovakia	XII	Paricutin to Quicksand
V	Daguerreotype to Epiphyte	XIII	Rabbits to Signaling
VI	Erosion to Geysers	XIV	Silk to Textiles
VII	Ghosts to House Plants	XV	Thailand to Volcanoes
VIII	Hudson to Korea	XVI	Wales to Zoos—Index

CONTRIBUTING ARTISTS

Dot and Sy Barlowe • Cornelius De Witt • E. Joseph Dreany • Bruno Frost
James Gordon Irving • Beth and Joe Krush • Harry Lazarus • Andre LeBlanc
H. Charles McBarron • Denny McMains • Harry McNaught
Ray Perlman • John Polgreen • Evelyn Urbanowich

Pauline Batchelder Adams • George Avison • Barry Bart • Ernie Barth • Charles Bellow
Eric Bender • Juanita Bennett • Merrit Berger • Robert D. Bezucha • William Bolin
Thelma Bowie • Matilda Breuer • S. Syd Brown • Peter Buchard • Louise Fulton Bush
Jim Caraway • Nino Carbe • Sam Citron • Gordon Clifton • Mel Crawford • Robert Doremus
Harry Daugherty • Rachel Taft Dixon • Olive Earle • Sydney F. Fletcher • F. Beaumont Fox
Rudolf Freund • Tibor Gergely • Douglas Gorsline • Hamilton Greene • Gerald Gregg
Marjorie Hartwell • Hans H. Helweg • Janice Holland • W. Ben Hunt
Arch and Miriam Hurford • Harper Johnson • Norman Jonsson • Matthew Kalmenoff
Janet Robson Kennedy • Paul Kinnear • Olga Kucera • Walter Kumme • John Leone
Kenneth E. Lowman • John Alan Maxwell • Jean McCammack • Shane Miller • Stina Nagel
Elizabeth Newhall • Gregory Orloff • Raymond Pease • Alice and Martin Provensen
Jerry Robinson • Feodor Rojankovsky • Roki • Mary Royt • Arnold W. Ryan
Arthur Sanford • Sam Savitts • William Sayles • Al Schmidt • Edwin Schmidt
Frederick E. Seyfarth • Robert Sherman • George Solonewitsch • Lionel Stern
Norton Stewart • Valerie Swenson • Gustaf Tenggren • William Thompson • Felix Traugott
Eileen Fox Vaughn • Herschel Wartik • Robert Weisman • Garth Williams

MAPS BY

Vincent Kotschar Jean Paul Tremblay
Carol Vinall Frederic Lorenzen
Rudolf von Siegl Francis Barkoczy

COVER ARTISTS
Ned Seidler • Ken Davies • Don Moss